AWAKENING THE REAL YOU
THE KEY TO HAPPINESS

to Judy, Kira and Sean
may you always live the beauty of harmony

and to Ray Lee
who did

RAY NEWMAN

Copyright 2004 TestBright
42 East Shore Trail, Sparta, NJ 07871
(973) 729-0025
ISBN# 0-9615247-8-2

CONTENTS

		PAGE
	PROLOGUE	*5*
1	*IT'S IN THE NATURE OF THINGS*	*9*
2	*THE REAL YOU*	*15*
3	*A MATTER OF PRINCIPLE*	*28*
4	*THE ASSAULT ON MIND BODY HARMONY*	*35*
5	*EMOTIONS*	*42*
6	*SPEAK UP, SPIT IT OUT*	*46*
7	*NEVER FEEL GUILTY AGAIN*	*62*
8	*DUTY: A MOST EVIL CONCEPT*	*74*
9	*CLASSIC CLASHES*	*80*
10	*YOU DID WANT A CHILD, DIDN'T YOU?*	*85*
11	*THE CRUELEST HOAX*	*90*
12	*BUT IS IT A CRIME?*	*94*
13	*THE DEFENSE*	*99*
14	*WHAT IS SUCCESS?*	*106*
	THE BIRTH OF RUPERT LYLE A SHORT STORY	*125*

PROLOGUE

I did not personally know the first human being to ever walk the planet Earth. But it would have been fascinating and enlightening to have done so.

What did he (or she) think about? Could he think in any way comparable to the way that we do? Did he ask questions of himself? And what type of questions? Did he wonder where he was? Where everyone else was? Did he realize he was alive? Did he wonder what life was all about?

And what about his feelings? Did he feel good about waking up in the morning? Did he look forward to things? Was he hopeful? Or did he feel lonely, anxious, afraid? Was he angry? And if so, at what, and why?

And perhaps most importantly, did he experience a long-term overall sense of pleasure and contentment and well-being? In other words, was he happy?

Of course, we have no way of knowing for certain. After all, he left no records, no written descriptions of his mental state. He was examined by no one. He took no psychological tests. But if I were to guess, I would think he was happy, and here's why: Happiness derives from a pattern of attaining one's values...that is, one's goals. One's rational values and goals. And being alone on the Earth, he must have acquired his rational values and goals or he could not have survived for very long. He must have acquired the food he needed to satisfy his hunger and his biological needs. He must have somehow found shelter from the elements and from the wild beasts around him who perceived him as a way to satisfy their hunger. In all likelihood, he found some companionship with some tamer animals. He probably saw the beauty of a mountainside, a waterfall, a sunset, a bird on the wing.

Now, to be sure, he could not experience many other sorts of pleasure...painting, sculpture, music (although he might have banged a stone with a stick), literature, human love. But I have to believe that in the sense that he survived, that he managed to acquire a measure of control over his life and to overcome the threats to his life, he must have felt a sense of efficacy, a measure of pride and of self-esteem. A feeling of living successfully.

A feeling of being happy. Throughout the ages, man has sought to discover and to understand what it takes to achieve the wonderfully rewarding feeling of being happy. Why some achieve it and others do not. Library and bookstore shelves are filled with a seemingly endless array of books that proclaim some insight into the mystery from all sorts of perspectives...emotional, psychological, financial, physical, spiritual.

And this book is yet another one. Another one that offers clues to happiness. But this one from a different perspective. *A natural one.* As you will see, this book examines the issue of happiness from the most basic and fundamental perspectives applicable to human beings and proves its points by reference to obvious facts in reality.

It is interesting to note that if you ask yourself why you are doing something, the ultimate answer will always be something like: "So that I will be happy."

For example:
- Q: Why do you go to work?
- A: To make money.
- Q: Why do you want to make money?
- A: To be financially able to buy things, like a new car.
- Q: Why do you want a new car?
- A: Because it looks and drives better.
- Q: Why do you want a car that looks and drives better.
- A: Because it will make me happy.

In other words, the goal of all our activity is to be happy. That has been, is and for all time will be universally true for all rational, mentally healthy, people. No wonder, then, the unrelenting quest for keys to happiness.

The ideas in this book are not all new to me. I have learned from others. I have added perspectives of my own. And the integration of the material and the form of presentation are peculiarly mine.

I can tell you that my realizing and implementing the ideas in this book on a daily basis changed my life. It has given me a greater sense of control over my life, my mental functioning, my feelings, the achievement of my goals. It has dramatically changed for the better my reactions, emotional and otherwise, to external influences. It has made me feel more harmonious with the natural world and has made me more comfortable with myself, with my own being. It has awakened in me my true self, and has allowed the real me to come alive.

And perhaps most importantly, and as a consequence of all of the above, it has made happiness easier to attain and maintain. I can now even find happiness in the discipline I use to acquire it, and in the pride I feel in being true to my ideas. Which means, being loyal and true to myself.

In other words, I (and you) can experience happiness in the search for it.

CHAPTER 1

IT'S IN THE NATURE OF THINGS

You are home and the doorbell rings. You open the front door and there is a deliveryman there holding an African Lily plant. A card attached to the plant indicates that it is a gift from a friend. You take the plant inside the house, admire it for a while, and then, in all likelihood, you ask yourself the following two questions:

>How much water does it need?
>How much sunlight should it get?

You have never owned an African Lily plant, you do not have a book on plants in the house, so you call the local florist.

"An African Lily plant?" the florist asks rhetorically. "Water it generously every other day and expose it to natural light."

Now that simple tale about a plant may be the most important story you will ever hear. It is the key to personal fulfillment, a rewarding life and happiness. Really, it is!

Let me prove that to you.

The two questions you asked yourself about the plant, regarding the amount of water and sunlight it ought get, reflect your awareness (consciously or subconsciously) that if the plant is to be healthy and survive, it must be treated in a certain way. That there is a proper course of action to take with regard to it. Too little, or too much, water or sunlight will harm the plant, perhaps kill it.

Now even though you may have never owned an African Lily plant and perhaps never even read or heard about it, you "know" that it is not an "anything goes" proposition, and that there is a right and a wrong way to treat the plant if you want the plant to blossom, to bloom, to flourish. Don't you?

And when the florist answered your questions about caring for the plant, without examining it, he was expressing, implicitly, a fundamental aspect of our world: every species in the Universe is something special, something unique. Every species has its own identity, its own nature, and if it is to survive, it must be treated in accordance with its nature. In philosophy, that is sometimes referred to as "The Law of Identity." A is A: things are what they are.

An African Lily plant, the florist knows, is not a Swordfern, a Crossandra or a Spotted Dieffenbachia. Every African Lily plant, the florist knows, has the same fundamental nature and each must be treated the same if it is to bloom. That is why he did not have to see nor examine your particular plant to know how it should be treated. An African Lily, after all, is an African Lily, and once you know the nature, and thus the needs, of one, you know them all.

You've done that yourself, haven't you? A friend gets a certain type of dog and you say something like, "Be sure to let it run around outdoors a lot, they like that." That is you espousing The Law of Identity.

One thing further about the plant. What you or I or anyone else, even the florist, subjectively thinks about how much water and sunlight are good for the African Lily, is irrelevant. Completely. The only determining factor, the one and only decider of what is or is not good for the plant, is the plant itself. The nature of the plant itself. Our personal opinions about how to treat the plant are correct only if...only if...they coincide with, if they reflect, the nature of the plant itself.

Is that not what education is all about, learning the nature of things in the world? It has been said that there is, ultimately, only one question: "What is it?" And the answer to that question, applied to everything we encounter, unlocks the mysteries of the world and serves as a guidepost for human action.

The points I have made to you about the African Lily plant are not new to you. You know them, though not necessarily in the terms in which I presented them.

But do you know that the very same points, the very same ideas, apply equally well to me and to you? To all human beings? Are you aware that even though we have different personalities, characters and temperaments, we all have the same nature? That we are members of a particular species of life and, like the African Lily plant, and every other living entity, we must be treated (and that includes the way we treat ourselves) and act in accordance with our nature if we are to survive and to bloom...that is, to be happy.

To act contrary to our nature, to deny The Law of Identity as it applies to us, is self-destructive. Literally. In every way...mentally, physically, psychologically, emotionally...we harm ourselves when we do not recognize our fundamental nature and/or fail to act in harmony with it. We restrain our potential, we inflict unnecessary pain and anguish upon ourselves, we miss fulfilling opportunities of life. We estrange ourselves from ourselves, we lose touch with who we are. We sublimate our real selves and live lives of lies. And as a consequence, we lose sight of the path to happiness.

The failure to act in harmony with our nature kills us. Or induces us to kill ourselves.

And here is yet another horror story: we have, each of us, not only not been taught to understand our nature and to act in harmony with it, but we have been repeatedly taught and encouraged to act against it!

The dominant, rampaging ideas in our society today are ideas that run contrary to our nature. Worse. Which attack our nature and, thereby, attack our lives as human beings and reduce, if not destroy, our chances of being happy.

I am not exaggerating, as you will see. The single most fundamental, most significant, barrier to our achieving personal happiness is our failure, on an individual level, to recognize our nature and to consistently act in harmony with it.

If life doesn't measure up to your expectations...if it often seems meaningless, pointless...if one day seems routinely like any other...if you feel out of control...if only occasionally do you feel a sense of exhilaration at being alive...it is probably due in major part to the fact that you are acting contrary to your nature. You are giving the African Lily plant, so to speak, too much or too little water and/or sunlight.

You have heard the horror story. Now, here is the antidote. If you choose to commit yourself to discovering your nature and abiding by it (and you can do that, since free will is part of your nature), you open the door to a fulfilling life, a rewarding and happy life far greater than you can probably now imagine. A life where each day is filled with challenges and rewards and where even failure is seen as bringing you a step closer to success. Nothing, of course, can guarantee that you will be happy. External factors over which you have no control can influence your life adversely.

But one thing is certain: if you fail to act in harmony with your nature on a consistent basis, you may experience moments of joy, but you will surely suffer bouts of unhappiness, misery and pain, a life that only infrequently exhibits the spark and passion for which we all yearn. Why? Because that is your nature, and your nature (reality) cannot and will not be denied.

Animals in this regard are blessed. They have a distinct advantage over us. They are programmed to instinctively act in accordance with their nature. The beaver builds the dam. The spider spins its web. The cat does not attempt to fly.

But we have no such instinct, no pre-set program. The glorious gift of free will is a two-edged sword. We have the unique advantage of choosing the course of our lives, but we can choose incorrectly, we can act against our interests (who hasn't?), we can walk into walls.

14

How important then is it for us, in our quest for happiness, to learn our nature and the nature of the world in which we live, and to pledge to ourselves an unswerving commitment to honor that nature by every choice we make, by every action we take.

Do you let the real you emerge on a daily, moment-to-moment basis, in every single facet of your life? Do you live to the fullest the very special, self-created and unique personality that is you? Do you exult in living *you?*

Do you know your nature as a human being?

CHAPTER 2

THE REAL YOU

There are many aspects to your nature as a human being with which, no doubt, you are already familiar, including:

 * You are confronted with a life and death alternative, which makes critical the decisions you make and the actions you take.

 * Your physical composition has distinct limitations and a vulnerability to certain viruses, bacteria, poisons, etc.

 * You have a free will which is not automatized and which is subject to loss of memory, errors in judgment and uncertainty.

 * You have a built-in set of emotions that reflect your ongoing assessment of reality (you feel an injustice has been committed against you, you feel angry; you believe your life is in danger, you feel fear, etc.).

 * You have the power to think conceptually and to reason.

These are commonly known aspects of the nature of human beings and they are not directly the subject of this book. But there is another vital aspect that is not frequently thought about and not well understood, though it is an aspect that touches and affects almost every facet of human life, and it is this:

> You are a composite of Mind and Body, two interrelated parts that continually affect each other, are dependent on each other, and must act in concert with each other for you to be a complete, and a completely functional, human being.

The Body is our physical being (a collection of skin and bones, muscles and corpuscles, and more) which, on its own, does not have the mechanism to implement action. Without a Mind, its own or someone else's, to guide it, it lays motionless for eternity.

The function of your Mind is to collect data about the world in which you live, process it, evaluate it, judge it, and then decide what action, if any, should be taken. The function of your Body is to implement that chosen course of action.

Every action you take every moment of every day of your life (other than certain internal involuntary actions, such as breathing and heart beating) should properly follow that very natural sequence: the Mind, consciously or otherwise, choosing the course of action, and the Body acting it out. The thinking portion of the process may take hours or years depending upon the complexity of the subject matter and the detail given to it. Or it may take milliseconds and occur so quickly that one isn't even aware that any thought at all was given to the matter. We see a lion on the loose and we instantly turn and run to shelter. Did we spend time thinking about the danger? Yes. We saw the image of the lion, we identified it as a danger to our life and we responded...that is, our Mind decided a course of action and directed our legs (that is, our Body) to act.

Human action is the physicalization of human thought. It is the bringing of the thought, the idea, into being. When you follow that sequence of "thought-action," you are in a state of Mind Body Harmony (MBH). You are functioning as your nature requires. You are whole and complete, an active, viable, intellectually independent, human being. You are you, all of you, roaring ahead on all cylinders.

Any severance to the "thought-action" sequence, whether affected by you or by someone or some others to you, is a Mind Body (MB) breach. It is a betrayal of your nature (when the breach is affected by you on yourself) or an assault on your nature (when the breach is affected by others on you).

Here is a very simple example: You and your best friends and I are in a room. It is a large, attractive room. The temperature is comfortable, the room is well lit. There are attractive paintings on the walls. Every possible comfort and convenience is there for you to enjoy: food, drink, television, books, stereo, etc.

I leave the room and lock the door. You cannot leave the room without my permission. How do you feel? At first, you might feel slightly amused with just a tinge of annoyance at being locked in. Then, after a while, you likely will feel progressively more upset, angry, hostile, even panicky. Your hands may sweat, your face may get flushed. Your heart may throb, your pulse rate may quicken. You may feel claustrophobic. You may become violent.

Why? You have every creature comfort, don't you? Do you want other things? Sunlamps, VCRs, movies...what? You can have them all. It will not matter. You will still be in a state of distress and discomfort and unhappiness because I have severed the connection between your Mind and your Body. If your Mind should decide that it wants to leave the room (something you feel you ought to be free to do), your Body cannot implement that action. Your Mind is, in that regard, helpless, impotent. It is a feeling and an awareness that your Mind has difficulty accepting. That it doesn't wish to accept. The human Mind needs to, and likes to, feel functional, competent, efficacious. It needs to, and likes to, feel that its decisions are meaningful and that they will be carried out. Since that is the Mind's primary function, it experiences an enormous sense of frustration when the link between it and the Body has been cut and its control over the Body lost.

When I lock you in the room, I have imposed an MB breach on you, and you feel pain. You have no alternative, no choice, in that regard if you are a healthy human being with a healthy Mind. Your nature has been attacked, your ability to act in accordance with your nature as a human being has been curtailed. The real you, a combination of Mind and Body, has been beheaded. Anxiety, anguish, pain and despair are some of nature's responses to this MB breach. And happiness is now outside your reach.

Notice that even should you have no immediate desire to leave the room, you will still feel discomfort simply from knowing that should you wish to leave, you cannot without my permission. Your Body, in this regard, is now subject to my Mind's choices and not yours. For you, that is an MB breach. And that is unnatural.

While you may never have experienced the feeling of being locked in a room, you can probably imagine it. Have you ever been stuck in an elevator that has stalled...and did you immediately begin to feel anxiety and have difficulty breathing? Have you ever been caught in a traffic jam that is not moving (even when there was no urgency to get somewhere on time and even though you were sitting in the car with a friend, munching on snacks and listening to your favorite music) and did you not begin to feel irritable and at some point begin cursing? I have. Do you remember the frantic agitated beeping of the horns in the cars behind you when it took you more than one moment to step on the gas when the light turned green...signals of agitation that leads to snarled faces, pointing fingers and, sometimes, violence? These are examples of MB breach and the pain and torment it can inflict.

When will the anxiety lift? When will you feel better? When I unlock the door and you are free to leave (even if you choose not to), when the elevator door opens and you can depart, when the traffic begins to move, when you regain greater control over your life. In other words, when MBH is restored...and the real you begins living again.

MBH is the key to happiness because it is natural. Reflect for a moment on your own life. Think about the times when you are happy, fulfillingly happy. When you truly feel vital and alive. When life seems sweeter than sweet. Are those not times when you are enjoying MBH? When you are doing what you deep down wish to be doing? When you are uncompromisingly acting out your Mind's wishes? When the real you is unshackled?

And is it not exactly those times when you are the most creative, the most productive? When you feel most self-assured, self-confident? When life seems meaningful, wondrous? Have you not thought at those times: "Can life always be like this? Can I always feel this way?" (Yes it can, and Yes you can.)

And the times you are unhappy. Are those not the times when you find yourself doing things you don't really wish to be doing...and sometimes not even knowing why you are doing them? Or not doing the things you really wish to be doing...and sometimes not even knowing why you are not doing them? Are those not the times when you feel helpless, pushed-around, less than fully human? When you are disappointed with life and, most importantly, with yourself?

MBH creates a unity, a sense of wholeness, within you because it brings together your two facets as a human being. When your Mind is doing what it is designed by nature to do and your Body is doing what your Mind is directing it to do, then you are functioning at your optimum, your ideal. The stage is then set for you to accomplish more, to enjoy more, to be more.

I am not speaking here about the propriety, the correctness, of what you are doing. It is in the province of morality, ethics, as to what course of action is good for you and what course of action is not. I am not dealing with that here. I am addressing something more fundamental (notice the second half of that word): the methodology by which you function. The mechanism, the system, you use to implement action. If your methodology is improper, then it matters little in the long run what course of action you take.

You will not achieve lasting happiness. You cannot achieve it; your nature does not permit it.

But if your methodology is proper (and by that I mean that you keep your Mind and Body harmoniously carrying out their natural functions), then happiness and personal fulfillment are possible for you...provided, among other things, that your choices and actions are good ones, morally speaking.

Because MBH permits you to function at your optimum, you will likely accomplish more. Which, in turn, will motivate you to work harder and to seek even greater goals. That, in turn, will likely result in greater successes, engendering further motivation. You will establish a reinforcing success/motivation cycle with virtually limitless potential.

The achievement of personal goals helps to develop a sense of glorious purpose and meaning to your life...a purpose and meaning that most human beings desperately seek but rarely find. Life opens up and seems benevolent. People are seen as good and worth befriending. Accomplishment is possible, happiness attainable. And to the extent happiness is achieved, you will enjoy a feeling of pride and a sense of self-esteem. You feel worthy and your life worth living.

When your Mind and Body are in Harmony, your life moves ahead on a straighter line. And thus further. Into areas you haven't been to before, pleasures you have not previously known, passions theretofore muted or unexpressed.

Classically, one exemplary attribute of a hero was that he or she lives in accordance with deeply-held principles and acts in accordance with them and the judgments and directions of his or her own Mind. The hero is not to be pushed around, his will not made subject to the will or the threats or demands of others. Staunch in his convictions, courageous to defend them, the hero refuses to surrender his spirit, the essence of his being. And because those attributes are so rare, the hero so frequently is a loner, seeming to walk to the beat of his own drum, untouchable.

Because the hero is so reliant on his own Mind, he seems not to need others in the way most others do. And that frequently makes him an outcast, envied by those few who retain the dream of living as he does and despised by those who see his life exposing the folly of the surrenders which they have made in their own lives.

Consider the sheriff (played by Gary Cooper) in the movie, "High Noon." He has undertaken, by accepting the job as sheriff, to do his best to defend the town against criminals. When the bad guys approach the town threatening to destroy it, he speaks with the townspeople asking for their help. Feeling threatened, they refuse to help, leaving him to alone defend their homes, their shops, their way of life. His wife beseeches him to leave the town with her, saying something to the effect of, "If they don't wish to fight, why should you?" He chooses to stay and fight, to live in accordance with his word, in accordance with the standards that he has set for his life. At the risk of his life.

That he defeats the bad guys is not what makes him a hero. He would have been a hero had he lost to them. What makes him a hero is his refusal to succumb to evil (as the townspeople do, to their everlasting shame), his refusal to abandon his ideals and to allow others to impose their will upon him. He refuses to abandon who he is and to live someone else's life.

The sheriff, true to his beliefs, inspires many of us. He shows us the way life, human life, ought be lived (perhaps the way we, subconsciously, would like to live it). He knows that the surrender of his principles (that is, his Mind) to expediency is no less a risk to his life than confronting the criminals could ever be. If he is to live, he chooses to live only as a human being should live: as a free, proud and independent soul. Although there is nothing in the story, as I recall, to suggest that the sheriff understood the significance of MBH, he understood it implicitly and he understood that he must live by what he deeply believes because that defines who he is. How many are there who do the same?

It is interesting, though sad, to note that many of today's "heroes" are more like the townspeople in "High Noon" than the sheriff. People who, for one excuse or another, fail to live by their principles, or who have no definitive principles to live by in the first place...or worse, who have principles that denigrate life and humanity and civility (witness the movies and television shows which heroize and glamorize the underworld). Today, it is they for whom we are asked to have sympathy and compassion. It is their suffering, we are led to believe, that makes them heroes. And the greater the suffering, the greater the hero's mantle is thrust upon them. No longer a person to look up to, contemporary heroes are more often those, we are told, we should not look down at.

It is interesting, too, that stubbornly holding on to your principles and refusing to compromise is generally thought of as a vice, when it is, in fact, a major virtue. To compromise a principle is to abandon it, to replace it with a watered down version...which itself is subject to being further watered down or surrendered when "the going gets tough." On the other hand, to hold onto a principle in the face of attack and danger is to announce the sincerity of your convictions, the value of the principle to your life, and the value of your life.

It is in the nature of the world we live in that what man requires, even minimally, to survive and to be happy, is not automatically provided to him. Food, clothing, shelter, education, entertainment, etc. must be actively acquired by man. They do not arrive at his doorstep each morning (unlike the Biblical tale of God delivering manna to the wandering Jews in the Sinai desert). Man must take action to get what he needs and wants...and he needs a Mind, either his or someone else's, to make choices and to direct his course of action. If he fails to use his own Mind, or uses it improperly, then he must rely on the Mind or Minds of others to survive. He has no choice in this regard. Survival requires action and action, meaningful action, requires mental forethought.

If an individual defaults in using his own Mind and acting upon his own Mind's choices and directions, he places himself at the mercy of another Mind, and we have seen throughout history, and continue to see today, the disastrous effects of that default. Political and social bullies, predators and defrauders of every ilk, breed upon, prey upon, those who have abandoned the use of their own Minds. They depend upon that happening, they rely on that happening. They know that their evil, anti-life ways will not be countenanced by many and to obtain the support, the admiration, the fear and the compliance that they seek, they urge the abandonment of individual thinking and play the deadly game of "follow the leader."

Think of the Holocaust. Think of the wanton slaughter of twelve million people, the plan to exterminate an entire race. Think of the concentration camps where men, women and children were gassed and burnt en masse. Were the tens of thousands of German soldiers who implemented that devastation all blatantly evil, devoid of any humanity and civility? (Germany, at the time, was one of the most "advanced" countries in the world.) Were the German people who countenanced Hitler's mania all so pathetically dispassionate about human life, deaf to the screaming cries of innocent children, blind to the hellish depths to which they had fallen? I don't think so. So what then allowed the most vile human behavior in the history of man to happen?

Those who study Hitler's rise in Germany during the 1930's know that he argued forcefully that he alone knew what was right for the German people and for Germany, that their education was unnecessary and that all they needed to do was listen and follow. In other words, he induced them to surrender the judgments and choices of their own Minds.

Think of Jonestown and the hundreds of mothers and fathers who poisoned their own children in the name of finding a better world and life. Were they all insane, delusional, madmen? Murderers of the worst type? I don't think so. They were mindless, having surrendered the judgments and choices of their own Minds to the will of another.

The mindless man is more like the unthinking animal than a functioning human being. With no thoughts and principles to guide him, such a man (or woman) is basically Body only. Inaction and thoughtless violence against others are his only living options. (There is also the option of death, which the parents at Jonestown also engaged in).

And the man who does think but does not act out his decisions will soon find his Mind feeling pointless, purposeless, functionless, and it will begin to shut down. Thinking takes effort and why make that effort when it doesn't lead to productive action?

* * * * * * * * * *

In olden days, the family or the tribe was not only the primary social unit, it was also the unit of survival. Confronted as they were with wild hordes of men and beasts, with little defense against them but brute strength, plagued by forces of nature over which they had no control, and with each man's consumption, in the absence of technology, limited to what he alone could produce, men understandably banded tightly together in the interest of their survival.

In the process, however, many foolishly surrendered the one aspect of themselves that survival demands: an independent Mind. They blindly accepted the authority of the group, or of the group's leader, they unthinkingly took unto themselves the duties and obligations extorted by the group, they placed the interest of the group above their own. In other words, they "deharmonized and desovereigntized" themselves.

It ought be clear now why a proper political system in touch with the nature of the world and of men would recognize the needs of its citizenry to enjoy MBH and affirm the right of all to "life, liberty and the pursuit of (their) happiness" and provide them with a noncoercive environment in which to live.

Today, many (most?) people continue the error of their forebears...seeing themselves not as individuals but as links in a social chain, concerned more with living up to the mores and preferences of the group than those of their own choosing, suppressing their individuality in their quest to get along, to be accepted, to be welcomed into the group (only to find they have lost their identity, their uniqueness, their passion for living, their soul). Few men consistently think for themselves or consistently act in accordance with their own independently chosen rational judgments. And of those who do, many do so guiltily (since that pattern of behavior unsettles the group and is seen as threatening by those who preach, at heart, the futility and folly of the individual spirit). The consequence is a half-hearted, burdened life, lacking conviction, devoid of direction, uncertain and despairing...with none of the passion that only a free-spirited, confident, imaginative, independent Mind can spark.

It has properly been stated that a human Mind cannot be forced. That is evidence of, and a tribute to, its natural state. But it can be surrendered.

CHAPTER 3

A MATTER OF PRINCIPLE

A few words are in order here about principles. What are they? Do we all need them? Do we all have them? How do we know what our principles are? Where did they come from? Are they the right ones to have?

A principle is a general and fundamental idea about life that serves as a guideline for living...an idea that can be applied to many situations and triggers the choices we make. Such as, "You should always be honest," or, "If you haven't got anything nice to say, don't say anything," or, "You should respect your mother and father."

Human beings have the unique capacity to conceive of principles and principles are incredibly valuable to man in his daily life. Imagine being at a job interview and you are asked a question, the truthful answer to which will preclude you, in all likelihood, from getting the job. You are unemployed, you are the sole support of your family and the bank has advised you that it is contemplating foreclosing on your home. You desperately need the job. Should you answer the question truthfully or should you give the false answer that will help you get the job?

Without principles to guide you, you would have to quickly ask yourself, and answer, a host of questions, including:

What moral obligation, if any, do you owe to your prospective employer?

Do the obligations to support your family preempt those you may owe to your prospective employer?

If you can do the job, what difference does a lie make?

Or, imagine you are driving your automobile on the way to that important interview and you accidentally hit someone. Should you stop to help the injured stranger and risk missing the interview and losing a chance at the job? And if you had been speeding and you run the risk of being arrested and spending time in jail, and being embarrassed and shamed before your family and friends, should you stop...or should you run?

Questions like these cannot be answered quickly. If you needed to answer them, and many others, before you answered, you would be paralyzed. And by the time you did come up with answers, the situation would have likely changed and there would probably be a whole rash of new questions to consider. Without principles to guide you, you would have no alternative but to resort to your feelings. Have you ever been asked why you did or did not do something and your reply was, "I don't really know, I just felt like it"? As you will see later, feelings (or emotions) play an important role in our lives, but they are not necessarily reliable guidelines for action. The principles you hold, the underlying ideas you hold about life and rights and wrongs, allow you to function quickly, consistently and, hopefully, efficiently.

Do we all have principles? Yes, because, as I have indicated, it would be virtually impossible to live successfully without them. And because it is in the nature of our Minds that we can think conceptually and in general terms and, in a real sense, that is what we are doing when we employ the idea of principles.

Many people think of principles as applying only to proper moral principles...like honesty and integrity. But, in fact, principles apply not only to so-called moral principles but also to any general idea that guides human action. So, for example, some hood might hold a principle something along the lines of "Get away with as much as you can whenever you can" or "Promises aren't worth the paper they aren't written on." Those, too, are principles. It is a mistake, therefore, to see somebody doing something unsocial or uncivilized or immoral and say, "That bloke has no principles." That bloke does have principles, just not the principles you have and admire.

Where do we get our principles? For most people, principles are adopted, consciously or subconsciously, in a grab-bag fashion...a few garnered from parents, some learned at school, a few heard from the pulpit, some taken from books, movies and plays, some from friends, etc. And from my observation, most principles are adopted without first-rate consideration. You hear something, it sounds right, and you adopt it as a principle to guide your actions (perhaps without even knowing that you have adopted it). It would be rare indeed for someone leaving a movie about Robin Hood to stop and say to himself or herself: "Let's see. Robin Hood stole money from the rich and gave it to the poor. Does that mean that it is acceptable for me to steal from some large corporation or from the home of some rich people I may be visiting and give it to some poor person...me? Do not the corporate owners and the rich people have property rights to their money? And is it moral for the poor to take money that they know, or have reason to believe, is stolen?

No. The likelihood is that the person leaving the theater would not ask any of those questions. He might feel good about what Robin Hood did and he might subconsciously adopt a principle something along the lines of "It's OK to take from those who have more than they need and give it to those who have less than they need." (Does not the welfare system have its roots in that principle?)

And because people adopt their principles without much consideration or questioning, the principles they adopt are usually vague, indefinite and ill-defined, and often contradictory (that is, it is extremely likely that an individual is holding in his Mind conflicting principles).

For example: Do you hold as a principle that one has a duty to, and should obey, the law? That is probably a principle you would pronounce if you saw some young teenagers stealing goods from a department store. "That is outrageous," you would probably say. "They should be caught and punished and taught a good lesson."

But do you ever drive on the highway in violation of the speed limit and then say something like, "Nothing wrong with that, everybody does it"?

Have you ever been overpaid change at a supermarket or not been charged for some item and said nothing, or found a wallet with someone's name in it but kept the money inside it, anyway?

Have you ever smoked in a non-smoking area, driven with an expired license, parked in a no-parking zone, spanked your children excessively? Have you ever used marijuana or other drugs?

Despite your principle of "you should obey the law," you will find endless rationalizations and excuses as to why it is OK for you not to obey the law. "It is acceptable to break the law if many others break it also." "If the law doesn't really involve a lot of other people, there is no need to follow it." "If you think the law is unfair, you don't have to obey it." Etc. In other words, you will redefine your principle as the circumstances change and in a way you feel convenient.

And it is easy for you to do so because your principle was not thought out deeply in advance of your adopting it.

Do you believe in freedom and also believe that a person may be drafted into the military against his will and ordered to risk his life in a war he doesn't believe in and be put in jail if he refuses to do so?

Do you believe that a person ought live up to the contracts he makes and pay his debts and also believe that he ought be allowed to file for bankruptcy and have his debts extinguished (even though he subsequently comes into money, becomes rich, and can afford to pay his debts)?

Do you believe one should always be honest, but wouldn't tell your spouse if you committed adultery?

If you hold any of those contradictions, you are neutralizing your principles and making them impotent. Inoperative. Valueless.

Is it any wonder that you will hear people say, "I did it but I don't know why," "I had no idea what to do in that situation," "Sometimes I do one thing, sometimes the exact opposite."

Here are a few of the advantages of living in accordance with well thought out principles:

1. You will be more in control of your life.

2. Life's decisions will be simpler for you.

3. You will have fewer self-doubts.

4. Your actions will be more reasoned and consistent.

5. You will enjoy the great pleasure and pride of being intellectually independent.

6. You will not feel guilty. (See Chapter 7)

7. You will sleep better.

Principles define who you are. Conflicting, contradictory principles reveal a conflicted, confused person living on shaky grounds. Such a person is unreliable, inconsistent, whimsical in approach, and to a great extent, unreachable and unknowable. Well-defined principles consistently applied reveal a person in control of himself or herself, visible for all to see, proud, dependable.

In the last chapter of this book, I tell the story of a young man who sets out to identify his principles, his goals, and who he is. It is an adventure we should all take. And retake from time to time.

CHAPTER 4

THE ASSAULT ON MIND BODY HARMONY

I stated earlier that as a rule we have not only not been taught to understand MBH and its importance in our lives, and to live our lives accordingly, but that we have been taught to embrace MB breaches. We have, as a society, gone even further. We have disdained MBH and those who practice it and ennobled MB breaches and those who suffer them.

Parents, the most influential force in the lives of most children, are among the leading purveyors of MB breaches. How often have you heard parents replying to their children's question, "Why should I do it?" with the Mind-destroying, "Because I said so, that's why!" That is telling the child to do what he is told to do for the simple reason that someone else's Mind dictates he or she should do it. Without a reason given to support the parent's orders, the implied message to the child is loud and clear: "Your Mind doesn't matter. What you think is not important. Stop thinking so much."

Giving a child a reason for the parent's decision at least sends the message that ideas very much matter, that they ought be the major influence in our decisions and in our actions. A child brought up with that lesson will have the confidence to make decisions for itself when old enough and the courage to live them out. (See Chapter 10)

Many parents stress the importance of being friendly with even distant members of the family (including aunts, uncles, cousins, etc.), with students in one's class and with neighbors. This, even when such people have not, by their behavior, earned such friendship. The urging to get along with others who are undeserving of such attention sends the message, again, that your Mind and your judgments do not matter (so why use it or make them?).

Parents also teach a bad lesson when they fail to show appropriate interest in, and support of, their children's activities and interests. That failure sends a message to a child that its judgments about living are not considered worthy or proper by those whom the child most respects and loves, and that message can impede the child's developing and maintaining MBH.

Schools also promote MB breaches. Some grade students on how well they "get along with others." And, no, there is no factoring into that grade the question as whether the "others" are deserving of being "gotten along with." The message to the students (generally, very impressionable younger students) is that "what you think doesn't matter, smile when you don't want to, get along when there is no reason to." Is it any wonder that that idea, implanted in the minds of youngsters, remains intact and difficult to extract even as the youngsters grow into maturity?

Another devastating tactic employed by many schools and teachers is to direct students to do things a certain way without explaining why it is the right way to do them. I recall that a friend of mine once asked his mathematics teacher why you "invert and multiply" when you divide by a fraction. The teacher hastily replied: "Because that's the way it works." "But I have difficulty doing something when it is not clear to me why I should do it," said my friend. "You're being disruptive," the teacher angrily replied, "I think you ought to leave the class for today." Again, the message is clear: "Your mind and the way it functions do not matter. It is not necessary that you (mentally) understand. What is important is that you (physically) do what another Mind (the teacher's) has told you to do."

There are many other examples of errors educators make that attack the idea of MBH. But perhaps the most significant error is that students, for the most part, are not taught how to think, not taught how to use their Minds properly so that their Minds can perform their natural function of directing action. What could be more important for a school to teach? What would be more important for a growing human to learn? Yet, few schools include logical thinking as part of their required courses. I have taught test preparation courses for the Law Schools Admissions Test (LSAT), the General Management Admission Test (GMAT) and the Graduate Record Examination Test (GRE), all of which test logical thinking, and few of the students have ever taken a course in logic. No wonder such students fall easy prey to the fallacy of the Appeal to Authority ("It's right because my parents say it is so, the teacher says so, a book I read says so, the public says so," etc.).

Have you ever been on a job and made a recommendation to your superior about how something could be handled more efficiently, less expensively, only to have your superior dismiss your recommendation out-of-hand with a "No, I don't think so, we've been doing it the other way for years." That is an appeal to tradition, your superior replacing his or her Mind with the Minds of people who implemented a certain practice years earlier. In all of these cases, the message is the same: your Mind, your thoughts, your ideas, do not matter.

The primary function of education is to develop a Mind's conceptual faculty, reasoning and judging powers, so that it will be in a position to carry out its function. How many students do we see graduating from high schools, even colleges, who cannot think for themselves? And those who do think for themselves are generally thought of as iconoclasts, troublemakers, rebels, stubborn anti-social outsiders. And they are, fighting as they are to live in harmony with their nature and resisting those who seek to animalize them.

Ministers tell us: "Judge not lest ye be judged." Yet the Mind must judge if it is to make decisions about whom to befriend, whom to have business dealings with, whom to entrust our children to, whom to love, whom to marry...and either it will judge but not act on those judgments, or it will refrain from judging and shut down. In either case, it is an MB breach with painful, even deadly, consequences.

Religions teach us to obey commandments...that is, to do or not to do certain things under threat of eternal damnation even when our Minds think otherwise. The son or daughter, who, contrary to a commandment, does not respect his or her sexually abusive parent is guilty of a sin, and must presumably pay the price for acting in accordance with his or her own judgment. What should the child do: abandon its Mind, or act counter to the teachings of its religion? Should a person follow a religion that urges the abandonment of one's Mind?

And should a person who obeys commandments out of fear of severe punishment be commended for so doing? Is that obedience reflective of who that person really is?

Some religions teach us that we are born evil, stained with mortal sin. But how can we properly be thought of as evil for actions taken not by us but by others before us? That is a failure to recognize the basis of responsibility and the relationship between one's Mind and one's Body...and that each individual Mind has free will and is independent (and not a part of some collective mental entity).

Some religions promote the ideas of fate and predestination...both of which fail to recognize the Mind's natural role in setting the course of our lives. After all, if we are fated to a certain life, why bother thinking, what would the purpose of the Mind be if the results relevant to our lives would be the same? And wouldn't we be fated to think a certain way anyway, so why bother making the effort? (I closed each radio and television show I broadcast with the expression "Ideas Move Man, Man Moves the World"...meant, in part, to counter those ideas.)

The whole thrust of religion is that our lives are subject to the wishes and demands of a God's Mind rather than our own.

Society is replete with examples of its fostering MB breaches...the most notable of which is the promotion of an array of duties we allegedly each owe to other members of society and to unborn future generations and is the price we must pay for the "privilege" of living in society. (See Chapters 8 and 11)

Another example of society's attack on MBH can be found in its teaching that man ought to compromise his principles in the interest of "the public good." Compromise may be an appropriate tactic in business negotiations, but it certainly has no place in regard to fundamental principles. To compromise a principle is to abandon it. To fail to live up to your principles in full, in toto, is to betray them. And yet society continues to beseech us to "take the middle ground" and not to be "so extreme" in our thoughts and actions. (See Chapter 3)

Since most of the things that man requires to live (food, clothing, shelter, etc.) are not automatically provided to him by nature, he must go out and get them. In that sense, for a man who wishes to live, acting in his own self-interest is a necessity and a virtue. Yet the concept of altruism (an idea which makes others the prime beneficiaries of your actions) dominates our society. Many surrender the judgments of their own Minds and their own desires so as to be socially acceptable.

The disdain with which the word "selfish" is thought of in our society is evidence of this attack on the human Mind. If the price demanded for acceptance or friendship is the surrender of MBH, the suppression of your thoughts, the concealment of your identity, then the price is too high, way too high!

The bombardment against MBH continues relentlessly. The Body has been placed in a preemptive position relative to the Mind (as witnessed by the prevalent "go by your guts" attitude, our pervasive view of sex as merely a bodily function, our emphasis on physicality in music and movies and the growing violence in our society). In

Chapter 13, I discuss some ways to defend against that bombardment.

CHAPTER 5

EMOTIONS

Another important way in which society attacks the idea of MBH is in its promotion of emotions as the appropriate decider of action. "Do as you feel," "Go with the flow, baby" and "Let it all hang out" are some of today's slogans for the attack on the Mind...and on the individual.

But emotions, contrary to public opinion, are not cognitive. They do not tell you what is going on out there, information you require in order to make intelligent decisions. Let me show you.

Imagine you and I are in a room. The door bursts open and a masked man points a gun at the two of us threatening to kill us. The man seems sincere, the gun looks real. You feel fear. At the same time, I feel great joy. How can that be?

You value your life, your life is threatened, you naturally feel fear. I recognize my brother, he is apparently recuperated from his serious illness and is out of the hospital, he kids around like this all the time, he is harmless. I am delighted he has come to visit and I feel great joy.

So, I tell you that it is my brother, he wouldn't hurt a fly and that you have nothing to fear. You believe me and your fear dissipates, replaced by a sense of relief. But the masked man removes his mask and it is not my brother. I have made a mistake and I tell you so. Now, you feel fear again, and I feel fear as well. Then a man comes into the room carrying a TV camera and smilingly says, "Candid Camera," and our fear subsides.

What's the point? Emotions are not a source of information about reality. They are automatized responses to assessments of reality. And because they are based on assessments of reality, their relevance is dependent on whether those assessments are accurate. If the assessment underlying an emotion is accurate, then the emotional response is appropriate. If the underlying assessment is mistaken, then the emotional response is inappropriate in the light of actual reality.

If you believe your life is threatened, you will feel fear even if you are mistaken and your life is, in fact, perfectly safe. My assessment that the masked man was my brother induced a sense of joy even though, in fact, my life was in danger.

How many have fallen in love only to find that love gone, after a while, as they came to find that the person they loved was not the person they thought he or she was? Was the feeling of love real? Yes, though not necessarily appropriate to the reality of the loved one's character, temperament, etc. Deciding with your heart alone is to gamble that the underlying assumptions conform to reality.

It is for this reason that one should not use emotions as the basis for important decisions and as guides to important actions...unless one first confirms that the assessments of reality that precede the emotions are correct. Nature has given us reasoning Minds, which, if we employ them correctly, can look at and evaluate reality without being clouded by emotion.

Perhaps the emotion that most contributes to an MB breach is fear. What more powerful emotion is there than this potentially paralyzing inhibitor of action? The Mind works best when it feels confident and efficacious, capable of dealing with the world, of attaining goals, etc. Failure is uncomfortable and unpleasant to the Mind. It is something the Mind seeks to avoid.

No wonder, then, that a human Mind may develop a dislike and fear of failure so strong, that it will shut down and refuse to do its job...that is, to direct action. And that is a self-imposed MB breach. You want to do something, you have determined it would be good for you to do it, but the fear of failing at the endeavor is so crippling that you do not attempt it.

There is another, and related, fear and it is the fear of disclosure. Here, we are fearful that the truth about ourselves will be disclosed, revealed, to others and to ourselves. There is a positive image that people have of us, say, and we are fearful that something we do, or do not do, will reveal that the image is ill founded. We have convinced ourselves of something about ourselves (our level of intelligence, courage, etc.) and we shy away from anything that might reveal that that evaluation is incorrect.

The problem here is that the image has become more important to many than the reality. The popular slogan, "Image is everything," reinforces that idea. To those who buy it, the image has ultimate value and reality has become the enemy and must be avoided at all costs. What better way to resist disclosure than by avoiding challenges and risks, refusing to be tested and playing it safe?

The solution to the problem is basic: reality is where we live and it cannot and will not be denied. And one aspect of that reality is that we are not omniscient. We can and in all likelihood will make mistakes during the course of our lives and that is not a reason for the Mind not to perform its natural function of making decisions and directing action. Life is action and inaction is death.

To accept reality is to accept the totality about ourselves...the good and the not-so- good, the smart and the not-so-smart...though it does not mean that we must necessarily like each and every part of that totality. Accepting ourselves is predicated on valuing our lives and wanting to live our lives to the fullest. And that means learning about ourselves, admitting the full reality of who we are, and always wanting to take purposeful action to improve and enrich ourselves.

CHAPTER 6

SPEAK UP, SPIT IT OUT

We've been told since we were kids to shut up.

"Hey, kid, you're only ten. What do you know? Keep quiet, would you? Kids should be seen but not heard."

But, you know, kids often do have good ideas, something smart to say. Not always, of course, but sometimes. The human brain is a marvelous instrument and after working for even a few years, can come up with more than just dribble and nonsense. Which is the way many adults characterize what kids say.

Why adults do that is an interesting thing. After all, they were kids at one time, too, and you would think they would remember that they had some good ideas back then. Have they all forgotten that? If they did, that wouldn't speak well of the minds of adults, would it?

But I don't think that they have forgotten. At least, not all of them. I think many adults feel that they are being pushed around...by supervisors at work, by spouses, by circumstances...and they are not being heard. Their opinions, it may seem to them, don't seem to matter much in the world. No one really seems to be listening.

So, they become frustrated. And out of that frustration, comes a need for power and control...power over their lives and control over those around them. What better place to start than to tell their kids to zip their lips, to do what they're told, to be seen but not heard.

Now, the impact on the kids is manifold. They begin to feel that they are stupid. After all, the people (parents) who presume to love them don't even want to hear what they have to say. They begin to feel that the world is a hostile place in which, to some extent, they don't belong or don't fit. They begin to believe that the best course of action is silence.

And so develops another crippling MB breach: children wanting to speak out, to voice an opinion, but being constrained not to do so. A chasm begins to develop between Mind and Body. Think one way, act another. Don't tell people what you really think, who you really are.

As they grow a bit older and are in their teens, kids obviously are old enough to have opinions and attitudes and views about things. Parents can no longer silence them as easily as they do younger kids, and so turn to a different message: "If you haven't got anything nice to say, don't say anything."

Notice that no definition is given as to what is "nice" and what isn't. When you're fifteen years old and your sister, say, asks you what you think of her new dress, is it "nice" to be honest and tell her that you think it's the wrong color for her complexion and it's a bit long for today's style and it would look a bit better without that sash, and that she should return it and find something better...or is that not "nice" and you should keep quiet? Or murmur something like, "It's OK, I guess," and change the subject?

It is not surprising, then, that many of those who reach adulthood do so with a fairly well developed notion that they should think twice before speaking out. And that notion gets reinforced in schools and at work where conforming to the norm is generally preferred and where self-expression is generally frowned upon.

One of my first jobs was for an attorney who shared office space with an insurance agency. One day, I was called in by the attorney with this complaint: apparently, I did not make it a habit to smile on the elevator at the gentleman who ran the insurance company (I'll call him Al). I told my boss that Al was a rude, crude, immoral boor and that I had no reason to act friendly toward him. "How you feel about him," said my boss, "is irrelevant. Get along or get out."

So, my silence on the elevator was interpreted as not being "nice" and I would lose my job if I didn't make nice and smile at someone who wasn't worthy of that smile. Notice that my boss did not dispute my assessment of Al's character. That didn't matter. I was wrong for implicitly expressing my negative feelings about him!

The Biblical admonition to "judge not lest ye be judged" adds another reason to be silent. After all, if judging someone puts one at risk of eternal punishment, it is not something many would risk doing.

Rampant in our society, too, is the idea that "you can't know anything for certain." Well, if there is no truth, no reality, then it would be a good idea to keep quiet, since what could you say that would have any serious meaning?

The Golden Rule ("Do unto others as you would have others do unto you") adds fuel to the fire. Perhaps most of us would rather hear something nice about ourselves...how smart, how good, how wonderful, we are...than something not nice about ourselves. So, if we take this rule seriously, only nice things will pass over our lips...and judgments and criticisms will lay dormant within our Minds.

* * * * * * * * * *

We live in a cause and effect world. Things happen in the world because some cause acts upon something and produces an effect. And the same is true of silence. Silence can serve as a cause and engender certain effects.

Silence will frequently be interpreted as acquiescence. Someone does something, you think it is wrong but you choose, for any one or more of a variety of reasons, to keep quiet. Silent. The other person is likely to equate your silence with agreement. After all, you didn't say anything, you did not object, you did not complain, goes this line of reasoning, so you must approve of it.

Thus silence may actually promote in others the very activity you believe is wrong. Not only are you not raising an objection to that action, in the hope that it may dissuade others from repeating it, but your silence promotes the recurrence of that action. The very thing you hoped would not happen!

Imagine your surprise and chagrin when after that action is repeated over and over again, and finally, unable to stand it any more, you do speak out and object (hard as that might be for you), what you hear in reply is something like this: "What's the problem? You've never objected before. I thought you approved." How you behave is a popular indicator of what you believe. As it should be, if you are not engaging in a Mind Body breach.

Another consequence of keeping quiet is that you will not be able to trust others. After all, if you are not saying what you really believe and how you really feel, you are likely to feel that others are probably doing the same. And thus you can no longer believe what you hear. When others pay you compliments, are they sincere, do they mean what they say? Or, are those compliments nothing more than a "do unto others" cover-up for some "un-nice" things people really feel about you? No way for you to know for certain, is there?

Ask others if they are sincere and they will tell you of course they are. But is that real or is it a "get along or get out" lie? Notice that you can no longer enjoy those compliments, those manifestations of love and affection and admiration, because they may not be real. Truth be known, they probably aren't, at times.

Biting your tongue and not rocking the boat are all akin to lies. Your life becomes a lie. By not revealing what you truly believe, you don a mask that hides your true identity, the real you. You choose to live in unreality...where there is nothing, of course. There are no values to achieve, no values to enjoy. Unreality is nonexistence and that is where lies place you.

And that is where so many choose to live because it appears to them that it is easier, safer, to live in unreality rather than in reality, where people judge you and what you do, and sometimes voice that judgment and make you feel bad. (Perhaps, as you should feel.)

But feeling bad isn't all bad. From that bad feeling we can learn something about ourselves, something we can give attention to, something we can change. Who is the one who is more beneficial to our lives? The liar who tells us what we want to hear, even though it may not be true, or the person who tells it to us the way it is? You decide.

Social lies...believing one thing and saying another, in the name of propriety, convention, tradition, correctness...are an insidious MB breach with all of the consequences that that breach engenders. In today's world, unfortunately, there are adverse consequences to speaking out, as well. You will likely lose friends, you will not be accepted into today's culture (perhaps that is not adverse), you may become isolated and that may trigger loneliness. At work, you may not get job promotions, deserved raises in pay or invitations to employee get-togethers. You will be talked about and laughed at behind your back, and that may hurt you (it shouldn't...think of who is doing the talking and the laughing). You will become the threat, the danger, to be avoided at all costs.

Is that too high a price to pay for retaining your identity, your integrity, your self-esteem, your life? Your quest for happiness? Only you can answer that for you!

* * * * * * * * * *

It is interesting to consider what type of person would tend to speak out and what type of person would choose to keep silent in situations where speaking out is likely to receive adverse social reaction.

Individualists, those who believe that shaping your own identity, your own personality and character, is man's greatest accomplishment, would tend to speak out. They would likely wish to express who they are, to be recognized for who they are and to be accepted, if at all, because of who they are. They would wish to judge and to be judged.

Collectivists, those who believe that they are fundamentally links in a social chain, generally derive their primary identity from membership in the group, and would tend to keep silent. To them, the interests and well being of the group supersede their own interests. They would likely be willing to subvert and to hide their true feelings in the interest of not ruffling feathers and rocking the group boat. They accept the unstated clause in the unwritten social contract: "I won't judge you nor say anything bad about you if you won't judge me nor say anything bad about me."

Another distinction between those who speak out and those who keep silent is in the Confidence Rating (CR). Those who are confident and secure about themselves would be more psychologically capable of hearing negative comments about themselves than those with a lower CR. In fact, those with very high CRs would be anxious to hear those comments since they could learn from them and make any appropriate changes to improve their behavior and their lives. An Academy Award-winning actress once told me that she preferred to get favorable reviews, of course, but would rather read unfavorable ones since she could learn more from them.

Related to the "individualist/collectivist" distinction noted above is the question of from whom we achieve our self-esteem. The individualist derives it from himself or herself. He (or she) knows that the most important judgment about himself is his own. What others think of him may be considered and evaluated, but the ultimate and significant judgment rests within himself.

The collectivist derives a substantial portion of his self-esteem from others. It is their compliments he seeks, their approval he courts. His self-esteem is, at least in part, a gift from others. Any wonder, then, that he is reluctant to risk losing that self-esteem by speaking out.

* * * * * * * * * *

Think of where we would be, where this country would be, if some people had not spoken out.

The Founding Fathers, to their everlasting credit, spoke out:

"We, the representatives of the United States of America...do...in the name, and by authority of the good people of these colonies, solemnly *publish and declare* (emphasis added), that these colonies are, and of right out to be, free..."

Where would we be if they had not spoken out against the wrongs and persecutions they perceived and if they had not been willing to risk "our lives, our fortunes, and our sacred honor"?

Where would this country be today, what level of abuses and violations of rights would still be perpetrated against blacks and others if Rosa Parks had not spoken out? Had she not said, in effect: "I refuse to move to the back of the bus, I refuse to accept what you are doing to me and to others. It is wrong, it must change, even if I must go to jail, or worse, to make it happen."

Where would we be today if millions of young men and women had not spoken out and enlisted in the military during World War II, risking their lives to halt the tyrannies unfolding around the globe? How many more would Hitler have killed? How many more would have burned in ovens?

And what is equally important, where would we be today if more had spoken out against the wrongs they witnessed, unwilling to sit by quietly in the face of evil?

* * * * * * * * * *

Speaking out is a potent way of showing your disagreement with something wrong that was said or done, but it is not the only way.

For example: If I think that the local butcher has adjusted his scales so that the "pound" of meat I get weighs less than the pound I am charged for, I could confront him with my beliefs and give him a chance to reply, to explain, to disprove what I believe. It may be that he is not aware of the scale's malfunctioning. Speaking out would be a civil thing for me to do.

Or, I could simply stop buying my meat at his shop and try to induce my friends not to buy there, either. Not give my money to the immoral, so to speak. That method of "speaking out" is not as clear since the butcher would have no way of knowing why I no longer patronize his shop. Is it because I think he is a cheat, is it because his prices are too high, is it because the location of his shop is not convenient, etc.?

Or, I could write a letter to the governmental agency that monitors such things and request that his scales be tested and, if found wanting, that he be fined and/or otherwise punished.

All of these ways, and others, are ways of speaking out. Some more powerful than others. It is for each person to choose his or her method of speaking out in any particular situation, his or her method of affecting change for the better.

* * * * * * * * * *

Notice, too, that because society's disdain about speaking out is incorrect, it creates a moral inversion when it is implemented.

Speak up when society thinks you should not and you become the threat, the villain, the immoral one. You are the one urged to amend your ways, the one shunned if you do not. It is you that is considered uncivil, the one without social graces.

And the person who did the wrong about which you voiced your disagreement, the one who should be condemned and held in society's disfavor, becomes the harmed one, the one to whose side society rushes, the one "entitled" to moral indignation.

How ironic! Civility and social graces should sensibly be predicated on what is a good way to live, the right way to live. And that, hopefully, would minimally include a commitment to honesty and to the truth. What a shame it would be (it is) for those notions to honor the untruth, the lie, as their standard of behavior. How pitifully shortsighted it would be (it is) to believe that the threads which hold society together can be woven of such frail social concepts.

The irrational doctrine of "say nothing if you have nothing nice to say" always wreaks its irrational consequences. It is a promoter of Mind Body disharmony. It abandons the good and nourishes the bad.

* * * * * * * * * *

Our legal system is based on the notion of fairness and equity. The person who does wrong and harms another should be seen for what and who he or she is and be made to pay the appropriate price. It is the legal system that is the true bulwark against oppression and injury, the true barrier between civility and degradation.

One key element of that judicial system is the subpoena power. A person who has information relative to the issue at hand may be subpoenaed, with a few exceptions of privilege, and be required to testify even against his or her best friend...under penalty of going to jail, if one refuses (or lies under oath).

The underlying reason for the subpoena power is that if one has information relative to a matter at hand, a moral person should wish to testify in the interest of promoting a just society and since refraining from testifying, and concealing that information, could lead to an unjust judgment.

Should not the same notions for the same reasons be encouraged in non-legal situations? In more casual, social situations? Should we not want justice and the good to prevail? And the bad to be punished?

* * * * * * * * * *

I have to wonder how many cases of adultery and divorce are related to this hesitation to speak out. Over time, hearing only nice things said about us, coupled with so many of us gaining our self-confidence from the opinions of others, can make our self-esteem inordinately fragile. We can become unable, and unwilling, to hear negative comments or criticisms.

And, from my observation, this certainly applies in the case of married couples (possibly the last place it should apply). How many husbands (and wives) are reluctant to express to their spouses their negative feelings about the way their marriage is going? Reluctant to suggest that their spouses are doing something wrong, unattractive, and that that something is impacting the way they feel about their spouse...and feel about their marriage?

On some level, acknowledging that a marriage is not going as well as expected or hoped for, may be seen as an admission of failure...and if there is one thing a human mind resists admitting, it is failure. Failure hurts psychologically and emotionally and intellectually.

On the other hand, acknowledging that a marriage has problems and wishing to discuss those problems is to imply the value and importance of the marriage and the hurt that will result if the marriage ends.

How many marriages would still be around today if the people in the marriage had been more open about their changing feelings, their concerns, their likes and dislikes? You know that when some of those couples go to a marriage counselor, one of the very first things the counselor will ask of them is, "Have you spoken to each other about your feelings?" So often, the true answer is "No" or "Very little." In the blind hope that what is wrong with the marriage will simply go away over time, many say nothing. Only to find that what they find wrong with the marriage not only has not gone away but has, in fact, worsened. And out of frustration, and out of a desire for some token of love and affection, and a need to feel that the world is a good place in which to live, they often turn to adultery.

When the counseling sessions are over, the couples will likely be advised to talk it out, to reveal to each other their true feelings, to be open and honest. Because that is the first step to a cure of what is ailing in the marriage, the best chance the marriage will return to the loving and nurturing and happy and fulfilling relationship it was intended to be.

* * * * * * * * * *

Let's talk heroes. Think about the heroes you admire in novels and on film. Is it not true that one trait common to almost all of them is that they are willing to stand up and speak out about their feelings and beliefs and to take the consequences for so doing?

Do we admire them so because somewhere deep inside each of us is a sense of the right way to live, the private yearning that we, too, might have the courage to do what those heroes do...damn the torpedoes, full speed ahead!...and free ourselves from socially-imposed and self-indulged bondage?

Want a hero? Look in the mirror. Make that person staring back at you, your hero. It is you and your choices, not society, that ultimately shape that person's character. You write the script for your own life. And that script can be as inspiring and as heroic as you, and you alone, choose to make it.

* * * * * * * * * *

One of the most damaging consequences of the MB breach generated by those who refuse to speak out is the subliminal acceptance of the idea that lying is proper. After all, if I say nothing when I wish to comment negatively about what you've said or done, I am engaging in a lie, am I not? And we are taught that that lie is noble, civil, a sign of being well mannered.

And so we lie, so often.

We lie on job applications...we exaggerate our experience because it will help us get the job and "they'll never know, anyway."

After we get the job, we lie often to our superiors, telling them what they wish to hear whether it is true or not. Otherwise, how else will we get promotions?

We tell police officers who have pulled us over for speeding that we weren't anywhere near the speed limit..."honest, officer"...when we know we were 15 mph over it.

We lie to the IRS about the amount of the tax-deductible contributions we put into the plate at church, and about our use of the company car for personal stuff, and about so many other things, if we think we can get away with it. Don't we?

To impress others, we lie about the amount of our income, how much we spent for that recently-acquired automobile, our age, and...worst of all, how happy we are.

(You're not lying about how often you do these things, are you?)

We are a society (a world) of liars. We are!

* * * * * * * * * *

To commit to knowing and speaking the truth at all times is to enter a truth dimension with priceless rewards:

    Enjoy the serene joy of revealing and expressing your true identity, of being more visible.
    Truly know thyself, as Socrates urged, and to thine own self be true, as Shakespeare implored.
    Lose forever the regrets of what you "could have said, should have said, might have said."
    Engage in more intimate and meaningful relationships that stand a much greater chance of enduring.
    Live a more exciting, passionate life.

Why is it that inside a courtroom society demands "the truth, the whole truth, and nothing but the truth," but one step outside the courtroom, society often shuns the truth teller and imposes proprieties, protocols, conventions and political correctness that often mask the truth? Is it because we seek justice only in the courtroom (Benjamin Disraeli noted: "justice is truth in action"), and not outside of it?

Are we afraid to hear the truth because our self-esteem is so fragile, our self-confidence so undeserved? Have we superseded the desire for justice with a desire for love and acceptance, even if they are based on false premises?

President Harry S. Truman had a reputation for "giving them hell." His reply: "I don't give them hell. I just tell the truth and they think it is hell."

I was fortunate to have a mother who told me, "God gave you a mouth, use it!" Many are not so blessed and live, to some extent, secret lives within themselves. Of all the MB breaches referred to in this book, perhaps none is more damaging, more enslaving, more anti-life, than the failure to speak out and reveal your true self.

In a poem I wrote recently listing some of life's "Sweet Sensations", I included:

> "To brim with courage when all's to lose,
> To proudly speak your own mind's views."

Sweet, indeed.

CHAPTER 7

NEVER FEEL GUILTY AGAIN

Who hasn't felt guilty at some time or another? Who hasn't felt that annoying, persistent, agitation that one didn't do what one should have done or that one did do what one shouldn't have done? All leading to a sense that one is foolish, stupid, bad, worthless.

The source of all guilt is a self-imposed MB breach. You believe one thing but act contrary to it. Your Body acts contrary to one of your Mind's deeply-held principles. Voila! You feel guilty.

And you cannot help but feel guilty. Guilt is your built-in, natural response when you choose to act contrary to your principles. Try to talk yourself out of it and you cannot. A friend tells you that you needn't feel guilty, but you do. The more you think about it, the greater the feeling of guilt.

And it does not matter whether the principle you hold is right or wrong, moral or immoral. Act against it and you feel guilty. Think you should telephone your parents once a week but you don't? Guilt! You don't believe in lying to your spouse, but you do? Guilt! You are a hit man for the underworld and you believe that those who do harm to "the family" should be eliminated, but victim in your gun sight, you feel compassion and you let your target live? Guilt! You can't help it.

So, the way to never feel guilty again is simple: Always act in accordance with your deeply-held principles. Always.

When you next feel guilty, stop and ask yourself which of your fundamental principles have you acted against. Examine the principle first...and closely...and consider whether it is, in fact, an appropriate principle to live by. If it is, then your action (or inaction) was wrong. If the principle is wrong, then it must be revised or it will likely lead to further guilt and chaos.

When analyzing any guilt situation to determine whether your principle or your action (inaction) is wrong, be certain to consider your guiding principle, the deeply-held principle which you may not readily acknowledge even to yourself.

For example: You find a wallet in the street with $500 in it. There is a card in the wallet that shows the name and address of the wallet's owner. You say that it is wrong to steal, to take from others what does not belong to you. But you pocket the money and either throw the wallet away or, out of a sense of magnanimity, return the empty wallet to the owner. And you experience a feeling of guilt...and worse perhaps, a loss of some self-esteem.

The first question you must ask yourself is: What is your guiding principle? Is it the "thou shalt not steal under any circumstances" principle? Or is it the "thou shalt not steal if you are likely to be caught" principle? Or is it the "thou shalt not steal unless it's a large amount" principle? For reasons of self-respect, we often do not acknowledge to ourselves our true guiding principle. (Of course, you must also be able to define your principle precisely. What does "steal" mean? Is finding and not returning money tantamount to stealing? What does "a large amount" mean? Etc.)

If you determine that you have, in fact, acted against one of your principles, what should you do? First, accept the fact that you have acted improperly. Second, do the best you can and make amends to, and ask forgiveness of, those you have wronged. And, third, vow never to impose an MB breach upon yourself again. And, get on with your life.

Why do people choose to act contrary to their principles? Generally for one or more of the following reasons:

* Succumbing to fear

* Holding ill-defined principles

* Holding contradictory principles

* Selling out for short-term gain.

It is worthwhile to consider these reasons in some depth.

SUCCUMBING TO FEAR: Probably the most inhibiting emotion we feel is fear. We experience fear when it is our evaluation of reality that we are in jeopardy of losing something, or not gaining something, we value. For example: we may fear criticism. We may see criticism as equatable with a loss of respect. If that loss appears inordinately harmful to us, we may experience fear. And that fear may induce us to temporarily abandon or compromise a principle (e.g., not speak out or take action that we consider important, in the face of the potential disapproval of others).

If the fear of losing a value is great enough, we may surrender our principles completely. After all, to function well, a human Mind must feel confident in its ability to think, to judge, to solve problems, to make decisions, to deal with others. Criticism subjects that confidence to a test. If the confidence is deserved, then the criticism will be seen as a potential source of additional knowledge and insight, and, therefore, itself a value. If, on the other hand, the confidence is not well deserved, then the criticism threatens to expose that sham and will be seen as something to be avoided at all costs, including the cost of one's principles.

Are you surprised that many will so easily sell out their principles? You shouldn't be. Sure, parents may tell us "to always be honest," or "to be respectful of others," but those principles are not defined and their application unclear. And they are often violated by those who teach them to us.

Schools also fail in this regard. I know of no school that includes in its curriculum the study of the function, the formation and the application of principles. Religious schools do refer to principles (e.g., the Ten Commandments are principles) but they are foisted on students by faith and fear (of eternal punishment). In other words, they are not reasoned out and thus must bypass the reasoning Mind to be accepted. I remember that as a child I once asked a very religious person why one should respect one's parents (as a Commandment decrees) even if the parents are abusive and immoral. His answer was classic: "Because the Lord has said so and you are not to question the wisdom of the Lord."

Many political leaders often merge their principles into one great overriding principle: "Do whatever reasonably has to be done to gain and retain office." (Sometimes the word "reasonably" is omitted.)

These and many other principles are vague and indefinite (see below) in the form expressed and cannot serve as active, functioning guidelines in our lives.

Thus, even if we "adopt" a principle from one of these sources, we frequently do not hold it as an absolute value in our lives. And thus the cost of betraying that principle ("abandoning" may be a better word than "betraying" since one must fully believe in a principle before one can betray it), so as to avoid unwelcome criticism and fear, may seem like a small price to pay.

Because the great joy and pride of living in accordance with one's principles has not been popularized, for many there is no contra-emotion to combat the fear. And few have the intellectual wherewithal to confront the fear with rational argument.

And thus develops the willingness to surrender the choices of one's Mind to the will, actual or perceived, of others, or to unreality.

HOLDING ILL-DEFINED PRINCIPLES: Because society does not promote the importance of principles and, to a great extent (as previously noted) downplays the importance of ideas, many people have not given sufficient thought to the principles they have chosen to live by. In fact, I suspect most people adopt their principles at random, not particularly knowing why they have chosen them. To many people, their principles simply "feel right." (See Chapter 5)

As a small test, stop reading this book for a few moments and see if you can identify the principal principles by which you live. Write them down, to give them some measure of specificity. Do your principles come readily to mind? Are they clear and concise? Do you hold them as active, guiding ideas?

For example: Did you write down, "Honesty is a virtue"? If so, how would you answer these questions?

1. Does being honest mean never telling a white lie? (How would you define "white lie"?)

2. Must you be honest in business affairs? (Or do you believe that business is business and has its own special set of principles?)

3. If a burglar asks you where you keep your family jewels, may you lie to the burglar without violating your principle?

4. May you lie to get a job you desperately need without violating your principle?

5. When, if ever, is it acceptable to lie if telling the truth will hurt someone you love?

6. Does your principle allow you to lie to your children? Your spouse? The IRS?

And so on. You get the idea. How clear in your Mind are the principles you have chosen to live by? How useful are they? Can you explain to yourself, to your children, what they precisely mean and why they are right? Can you turn to them and rely upon them confidently when an important decision must be made? Are your decisions, based on those principles, consistent?

Or are you likely to find that you sometimes (or often) feel guilty after you have made an important decision...a feeling that indicates that you have, in fact, chosen to act against a deeply held principle? (Why would you do that if you fully understand why that principle is right?)

That is the likely, frequent, result when your principles are not well defined. But don't feel guilty about that! Your parents, your teachers, have probably not taught you well in this regard. Were you ever taught that you need principles to live by? Were you taught how to consider alternative principles and on what basis to decide which principles are moral and right? Were you ever told that a principle you have adopted which you cannot prove to be right is no better than the reverse principle which you didn't choose? Has the importance of ideas been stressed in your life?

Or have you, instead, been taught that there are no truths, no black and whites, no rights and wrongs? Have you ever heard someone argue that, "It may be true for you, but it's not true for me"? Have you been told to trust your feelings, to rely on instincts (of which there are none), to follow the crowd's lead, to stop thinking so much?

In a commencement address at the University of Cincinnati some years after he had returned from the Moon, Neil Armstrong (who, I think, should have known better) said:

"Truth is seldom absolute. It's more often dependent on the perspective of the observer. Truth can best be described as the best currently available description. And certainty is exclusively the property of the freshman."

Of course, if Mr. Armstrong is correct, he couldn't be certain that what he was saying was true, either. Could he?

How exactly did Mr. Armstrong make it to the Moon and back? Was it due to the truth, the knowledge which we had about the Earth's gravitational pull, and the Moon's gravity, and how rockets work...or was it just dumb luck, pure coincidence, good fortune, that his spaceship happened to land on the Moon and then, somehow, mysteriously, took off and deposited Mr. Armstrong back on Earth?

To say that nothing can be known for certain, a common claim these days, is either to believe that there is no truth, no reality, or that the human consciousness, the human Mind, is incapable of perceiving and knowing it. To believe the former, that there is no reality, makes the idea of life and living, meaningless. If there is no reality, then you do not exist either, there is nothing, and the question of life and how to live it becomes irrelevant. Who would ask it?

If you believe the latter...that there is a reality but your Mind is incapable of knowing it...then living becomes impossible. From the moment you awoke in the morning (how would you know it was morning?), there would be no way that you could sensibly do anything that requires a choice. What would you eat, the cereal or the bowl? And how could you tell one from the other? Would you walk out the door or out the window, and how would you know why you wanted to walk out?

The deeper significance behind the statement, "You can't know anything for certain," is more potentially destructive of the safety and well being of this planet than any thermonuclear weapon could ever be. One could take steps to counter the dangers of a nuclear blast, but there are no steps to take if you have accepted the idea that knowledge is impossible.

That Mr. Armstrong should seek to purvey his anti-reality, anti-knowledge, anti-life, ideas in a university, a place presumably dedicated to knowledge (and he is not alone in so doing, by any means), signifies the extent to which that philosophical poison has spread. If Mr. Armstrong is right, that there is no certainty (and only naive, unknowledgeable freshmen believe otherwise), what would be the point of having a university?

Is it any wonder that for those people who believe there is little, if any, certainty in the world, the idea of thinking about, proving, adopting and holding on to principles, holds little value?

HOLDING CONTRADICTORY PRINCIPLES: For all of the reasons mentioned above, most people will likely hold contradictory principles. Because the principles they have adopted were adopted at random, some picked up here and some there, it is no wonder that those principles do not form an integrated, harmonious whole. Think not?

Consider: Do you know anyone who believes man ought to be free but owes a duty to serve in the military when his country calls? The military draft is antithetical to freedom since you are being forced to risk your life, your most precious value, because others have decided that you should do so. You are being forced to spend time away from your career and family because others have decided that that is a sacrifice you must make.

After I had been drafted into the U.S. Army and sent to Korea, I asked a sergeant what I would be fighting for. "Freedom," he told me, "you would be fighting to protect your freedom." I asked him if he saw any contradiction in the idea that I was being forced (having been drafted) to fight for my freedom. He did not. Nor would most people, I suspect.

Do you know anyone who believes in the idea of property rights...that what is yours is yours to dispose of as you see fit...yet supports the welfare system under which billions of dollars are taken away annually from some people (by force, under threat of fine and/or imprisonment) and given to others? Is that not a violation of the concept of property rights (which is predicated on the notion that you own your own life and the product of your labor)? Can you, at the same time, own and not own your own life? If you think so, you had better take it up with Mr. Aristotle, the author of The Law of Noncontradiction: "Something cannot both be and not be the same thing at the same time and in the same respect." Either you have property rights or you do not. Either you are free or you are not. And try as hard as others might, no one should be able to convince you otherwise.

For ideas to be meaningful and useful, they must be integrated into a harmonious whole without contradiction (or else, which idea preempts which and which idea would you follow?). Each idea should complement and reinforce the others.

If you are the type of person who frequently has difficulty making decisions on important matters, if you sometimes find that you are incapable of making any decision at all and have become what I refer to as an S. O. F. (Sitter on the Fence), then it may well be...likely be...that you are holding contradictory principles. And holding contradictory principles is equivalent to holding no principles at all.

SELL-OUT FOR SHORT-TERM GAIN: Many people choose to act contrary to their principles in order to grab what appears to be an imminent benefit. Unlike animals, man does not live range-of-the-moment. Because of his conceptual faculty, man has the option of choosing long-range goals that will represent substantial rewards in his life, rather than the more temporary rewards achieved short-range. In that sense, the expression, "something good is worth waiting for," is true because, as a rule, something good takes a while to accomplish. It takes concentration, determination, discipline and persistence. And not many are willing to expend the mental effort that those qualities demand.

Thus the sell-out for the bird in the hand, even if it is a dead chicken.

The primary problem with selling out for short-term gain is the downside of living a life without strong, moral guiding principles. That leaves you uncertain as to what course of action to follow in many situations, subjects you to the pain of guilt, lack of self-confidence, loss of optimism about, and passion for, living...and, perhaps most importantly, the loss of a signature identity that is *you*.

We have become a range-of-the-moment society. Quick and easy pleasures, rather than long-range happiness. Immediate gratification rather than far-sighted planning. Tomorrow, many believe, will take care of itself. But it won't, unless we put tomorrow's goals into motion today.

Notice that the four primary reasons that I have given as to why so many people do not live consistently with their principles are, to a great extent, interrelated. If a person turns away from his basic principles and chooses not to speak out because of fear of rejection, then he is, in a sense, opting for a short-range gain...to live the moment without fear. And that individual is probably also holding contradictory principles. On the one hand, he may be holding a principle that honesty is a virtue. But when he lies out of fear of rejection, then he is acting on another principle: honesty is not a virtue if it may disturb others. If you are honest only when others agree with you, then honesty is not an active, viable, potent principle in your life.

And all of these reasons for acting contrary to underlying principles are supported by the failure to appreciate the ultimate devastating consequence of not living in accordance with well-defined principles: the loss of the potential for happiness.

It is worthwhile to keep the reasons why you may act contrary to your principles categorized the way I have indicated. It makes it easier to focus on why you are doing what you are doing when you abandon, disregard or contravene your basic principles. It will help you to understand why you feel guilty when you do, and...here's the payoff...it will help you to correct your error and to develop, practice and maintain MBH.

CHAPTER 8

DUTY: A MOST EVIL CONCEPT

It should now be clear why duty is one of the most evil and damaging concepts ever conceived by man.

Duty is an obligation. Whether it be duty to parents, to country, to society, to future generations or to whomever or whatever, duty is something you presumably must do whether you want to or not, whether you think it is right for you to do or not, whether you think it is moral or not, whether you think it is good for you or not. Duty is an obligation imposed upon you by others, by the will of others, past or present.

And that is why it is evil. Because it negates your Mind. It sterilizes your Mind. It seeks to bypass your Mind, to make it ineffective and meaningless. And it is thus a major attack on MBH.

Since your Mind is the proper natural decider of your actions, and your actions determine to an overwhelming extent the quality and character of your life, you can see that duty is a direct assault on your life as a human being. Duty would have you live your life without the use of your Mind. What more insidious concept could there be: that you live your life as a corpse, a Body without a functioning Mind?

What is doubly onerous about the concept of duty is that it is often "sold" under an alleged noble banner. Something like, "Doing good for the welfare and benefit of others." We all have a moral duty, we are told, to care for the indigent, the ill, the impoverished, the incapacitated, the less fortunate, the children, the elderly, etc. Their needs, we are taught, are a claim upon our lives. We must do what others need us to do whether we wish to do so or not. We have no choice, we are admonished, in this regard. We are members of society and we have a duty to support others. It is inhumane, it is preached, for us to deny our obligations to others. God or government, we are told, will punish us if we fail to do our "noble" duty.

(I accidentally typed the words "a moral" in the fourth line of the preceding paragraph as "amoral." Or was it accidental? Incidentally, is there a greater oxymoron than "moral duty"?)

In the United States, an entire welfare system has been established on this alleged banner of nobility. And so successfully has it been marketed, that today very few question the nobility of welfare, just the value or the desired quantity of it. The principle that self-sacrifice is righteous and self-concern is immoral is so generally accepted as proper that the mere questioning of it is seen as a moral flaw.

But it is the reverse that is true. Self-concern is a necessity and a moral virtue because survival is not guaranteed to us. Man requires a host of things if he is to survive and to be happy. Unless he becomes the ward of another or parasitically lives off of others (as robbers and leeches do), he has no alternative, if he wishes to live as a human being, but to act in his own interest. And if anything in a true sense is inhumane, it is the idea of duty...promoted socially by so many who then use government force to impose it politically.

In a philosophy class I taught, a student asked me why I had stated that all of the Biblical commandments were anti-life. Some of the commandments, she believed, "thou shalt not steal," "thou shalt not kill," and "thou shalt not bear false witness," are quite good. In what way, she asked me, are they anti-life?

The commandments are anti-life, I told her, precisely because they are commandments...requiring that you do something, presumably desired by an alleged higher intelligence, under threat of eternal damnation. There are, I explained, only two ways to deal with a human being: through his (or her) Mind, by persuasion, or through his (or her) Body, by force. The former way (persuasion) conforms to the nature of a human being and the function of the Mind to rationally make decisions and direct a course of action. The latter way (force) chooses to bypass the Mind and denies its nature.

Notice, too, that the commandments are too vague to effectively serve as guiding principles. What does "thou shalt not kill"" mean? Does it mean, "thou shalt not murder?" Does it proscribe killing in self-defense? Or to protect the life of a loved one? Is it a prohibition against capital punishment? Against euthanasia? Is it meant to restrict the killing of animals? Or of growing vegetables?

And what does "thou shalt honor thy father and mother" mean? Should they be honored if they have been physically or mentally or sexually abusive? If they are immoral? If they are evil?

Years ago at a social gathering, I "invented" a game: "Commandments." The game was simple. Each person, in turn, stood up and confessed to the number of the Old Testament commandments he or she had ever violated. The average for that very respectable, responsible, educated, group was seven. At the time, I was surprised at how high that number was. But I have come to understand that codes of morality cannot, fortunately, be easily imposed on people via commandments, but must, if at all, be adopted freely and intentionally by each individual Mind.

There are repeated calls in the United States for the passage of a "national service" bill which would require young men and women to devote some period of time (in some proposals, up to two years) in so-called "social service." Social service would include a whole array of projects designed and directed by the government to solve some of this country's perceived social and economic problems.

But forced national service (like forced military service) violates an individual's right to live his life in accordance with the decisions of his own Mind and in furtherance of the goals and dreams which his Mind has chosen to pursue for the purpose of attaining happiness. And if indeed there are problems which the government is properly seeking to correct, then it ought approach these young men and women, these young humans, through their Minds...that is, seek to convince them that they ought sign up for a particular project because it is in their interest to do so. After all, who would want to serve a country that does not recognize one's freedom, one's humanness?

It is worth considering whether some people relish the notion of duty because it relieves them of the responsibility of making their own choices about what course of action to follow. To them, presumably, life is easier if others make important decisions for them. And, they feel, they need not feel blame if they subsequently discover that what they did was not appropriate, since it wasn't their decision to do it, anyway.

Making your own decisions is pleasurable and desirable if you have the psychological courage to assume self-responsibility...which may, at times, require the acceptance of the idea that your decision was the wrong one, and failed. There are many who are not self-assured enough, not self-confident enough, to withstand failure and what appears to them to be an assault on their intelligence and their "living ability."

The individual who enjoys MBH, and who seeks constantly to make that Harmony a cornerstone of his life, understands that the concept of MBH means more than merely the Mind and the Body functioning harmoniously with each other. It also means that the Mind and the Body are each acting in harmony with their nature. Not occasionally, but consistently, all of the time, in regard to all matters. The Mind of the Harmony-seeking individual knows that it is fallible, that it can and does make errors of fact and errors of judgment, that it does not automatically know the right answers to all of the questions it will face, that it does not automatically know the right action to take in every situation. It knows, too, that it must use the one thing that nature has given to it to find the right answers: its capacity to conceptualize and to reason.

This is not to suggest that man must make mistakes. He need not. Perfection is not metaphysically impossible to man, though it is extremely difficult to achieve in any one area of activity, no less over an active lifetime. Perfection in whatever one does requires the full focus of one's mental capacities, dedication and perseverance. It is work, but it is achievable.

And if one meets those demanding standards for perfection and still falls short and makes mistakes, there is no need to suffer a loss of confidence or self-esteem. Man must deal honestly with reality, including the reality of his own fallibility.

Notice, too, that it is our fallibility that engenders a sense of pride when we have chosen and acted properly and successfully. There could be no pride if we were infallible; there could be no joy in personal achievement if we could do nothing but achieve. Our fallibility is an integral part of the mountain we must climb if we are to succeed. Knowing that we are fallible, and why we are, are two of the smartest and most rewarding things we can ever learn about ourselves.

CHAPTER 9

CLASSIC CLASHES

It was Plato who was the earliest major contributor to the idea of an MB breach. Plato came up with the idea that there were in fact two worlds: the noumenal world (or the world of Forms) which, he claimed, is in essence the real world, the world where ideas exist in their pure form, and the phenomenal (this) world where man lives and which is only a reflection (and a bad one, at that) of the noumenal world.

The noumenal world is associated with the Mind, where ideas "live." The phenomenal world is associated with the Body, where ideas are "lived out." According to Plato, when ideas are lived out, they lose their purity and their true meaning and application, and they become diseased and distorted. In his famous Allegory of the Cave, Plato related the "reality" we think we see in the phenomenal world to shadows on a wall, mere images of the real thing.

Thus Plato sets up a duality. Two worlds at odds with each other:

    * One world, not known to most of us (Plato claimed it was known to him). Here, true ideas, but not man, exist.

    * The other world, this world, where man, but not true ideas, lives.

You have heard of this duality in a number of ways. Has someone ever said to you, "That is good in theory but not in practice"? That is Plato's dual world. To those who foster this conflict, the ideal exists in our Minds only and is not found in the world in which we live. The practical, on the other hand, is opposed to the ideal and is the way we live our lives in a physical, Body, sense.

Now, this conflict is absurd. What would make a theory good, if it could not be implemented in this world where we live? What would be ideal or good about it?

Well, you might say, it is ideal in the ideal world, in another world. Do you have any proof that another world exists? Is there any reason for you to accept Plato's duality? Notice, that by accepting his duality, you would be implicitly acknowledging that this world is not the real world, not the best world. That it is a mere shadow of what the real world is, not a good enough world.

I leave it to psychologists, sociologists and others to enumerate the disastrous effects that such an attitude can and does have on those who believe that they are shackled to a second-rate world. I leave it to others to tell you the number of those who have destroyed themselves to escape the anguish of a perceived unrewarding, meaningless, vacuous, distorted life.

Have you heard of the supposed conflict between the moral and the practical? The moral code, the ideal collection of ideas, allegedly exists in our Minds only. But, the conflict-promoters say, the moral code is not practical and the Body must live in accordance with what is practical. With what works "down here on Earth."

But, again, why would something be considered moral, pro-life, for man if it is not practical, if it doesn't work, in the place where man lives?

Have you heard of the supposed conflict between love and sex? Love...beautiful love...say the purveyors of this conflict, exists in our Minds only and is good; sex, they allege, is what our Body only indulges in and is bad, dirty, revealing a less-than-honorable side to our being. Religions, perhaps the major promoters of MB breaches, have traditionally sought to extol the concept of love while characterizing sex as a vulgar expression of the base and worst within us. (Is that why the ministers of some religions renounce sex?)

It is for good reason that Plato is referred to as "the father of religion," for it was his two-world duality that religions took and popularized as the foundation of their philosophies.

Yet what is sex? At times, it may be a predominantly physical activity. But man is physical and satisfying that aspect of himself is worthy and in no sense, degrading. It may also be an expression of love, the most intense way of bringing a mental idea, love, into physical form, a celebration of life and not an enemy of it.

Have you ever heard of the supposed conflict between ambition and greed? Ambition, the desire to get ahead, to do more and to achieve, is generally considered to be something good, but the desire for the earthly rewards of ambition and effort, including money, is considered something bad.

The spirit, the Mind, we are taught, is divine. The Body, we are told, is stained with mortal sin and is latently evil. Our Minds and our Bodies are at war with each other, they say, and presumably the war won't end until our lives end.

There is the classic alleged Mind Body conflict between reason and emotion. "Are you going to decide this with your Mind or with your heart?"...as if one of your heart's functions is to decide issues and determine action. Hearts are blood pumpers. I wrote earlier about the failure to understand what emotions are. Deciding with your heart is deciding emotionally. It is deciding without known and proven reasons to guide you, deciding by feelings.

The person who fails to use reason as his sole guide to action is indulging in another form of MB breach. Reason, and reason alone, provides the factual information that the Mind needs to evaluate reality and make its decisions. Every other alleged basis of knowledge (instincts, intuition, revelation, clairvoyance) is, in fact, just another word for feelings (emotions). Which is why they are not reliable indicators of truth. The person who turns away from reason at any time is turning to his Body to make the decisions that his Mind ought be making.

There is a personality associated with Mind Body clashes that is worth referring to in this chapter. It is the type of person who professes great admiration of, and devotion to, ideas, but who continuously makes decisions on the basis of feelings and what he or she perceives as the practical. In other words, this person mentally purports to accept ideas but physically rejects them and thus engages in a most insidious deception and cover-up and an MB breach of the worst order. There are many in our society who recognize that the outward, explicit rejection of ideas would be generally unacceptable, and thus believe an MBH masquerade to be "practical." (How ironic!) It isn't, anymore than any mindless activity is or could be.

The only practical human method of living is to appreciate that thought precedes action, that thought and action can and must be harmonious and that human progress and happiness are predicated upon humans being human...that is, living in accordance with their identity, which means living in accordance with their nature, which means living as an integrated whole, Mind and Body, Body and Soul, rejecting each and every form of MB breach for the poison, the destroyer of life, and the barrier to happiness, that it is.

CHAPTER 10

YOU DID WANT A CHILD, DIDN'T YOU?

The need for MBH is significant in the life of every individual, including that of a child. From the first moment of birth, the infant child's Mind begins to take on the activities that it and it alone is designed to do...the acquisition of knowledge, the making of decisions and the directing of the Body as to what course of action to follow.

We see in very young children, this thirst for knowledge. "Why is the sky blue?" may seem like an innocent and meaningless question to some, but it is, in fact, indicative of a healthy Mind beginning its quest for knowledge. It is as if the young Mind is already cognizant of the fact that it needs data upon which to base its decisions and judgments. Does this reflect an early-developed curiosity? Perhaps. The seeking and acquisition of data is, after all, an integral part of the functioning of the human Mind.

Similarly, the making of decisions. What parent will not tell you that his or her infant child has preferences, likes and dislikes, and makes choices even at the tenderest of years.

Similarly, the desire to act in accordance with the judgments of one's own Mind. What parent will not tell you that his or her child does not like to be told what to do, when to eat, what to eat, what toys to play with, how quiet to be, when to go to sleep, etc.

The need for MBH is natural for even very young children. For a parent to fulfill his or her responsibilities to the child, and for a parent to be deemed successful as a parent, the parent ought promote the development of the child's MBH at every opportunity. No matter what else the parent does, if the parent defaults in this critical area, if the parent fails to recognize that the child needs, by its nature, to think for itself and to act on its thoughts...a pattern which is vital to its long-term happiness...if the parent teaches the child that the decisions of its Mind are not of value...then the parent cannot consider its parenting a success and would indeed be contributorily responsible for the guaranteed adverse consequences to come.

Consequences, like a child growing up to believe that thinking is not all that important since it has to do many, many things regardless of what it thinks, that its Mind is not in control of its Body (so why bother learning and thinking?), that its Body ought listen to the dictates of others (since it must be, apparently, not capable of making its own decisions), that life is malevolent, and so on.

In the area of teaching, I can think of nothing more valuable that a parent can teach a child, whether explicitly or implicitly through action, than that the child's Mind is of enormous value and the engine of its life, that MBH is the key to living as a human being, the key to happiness.

When I stress the importance of MBH, I am not suggesting in any way that a child ought be free to do whatever it wants to do (any more than that interpretation ought be given to the call for MBH in adults). No one has the right to deny the MBH of another. Certainly, if the child is damaging the property of others, or causing or potentially causing damage or injury to himself or to others, then the child should be stopped from so doing. What MBH says is that absent these considerations, great liberty ought be given the child to think for itself and to follow through on its thoughts...in the hope of helping to develop a Mind that relishes thinking for itself, thinking that the world is benevolent (that is, success and enjoyment are attainable), and enjoying the pride of a chosen chore or job well done. The reward to the parents is the healthy development of a human Mind, the most wondrous thing that nature ever created.

How ironic it is that the virtue of desiring and maintaining MBH is the source of so much dispute and conflict between parent and child. How often is it, when you see a parent and child feuding, that what you are witnessing is a clash of MBH's...a parent wanting to do one thing (rest and watch television, for example) and the child wanting to do something else (like running around the room, watching a different show, etc.)? Or what you are witnessing is the parent demanding that the child do what it wants the child to do, attempting to insert its Mind in place of the child's Mind in the child's Mind Body configuration. The child, frequently (and hopefully), resists. Crying, throwing a tantrum and the like are the child's way of expressing, without ever having read this book, its need and longing for MBH.

And the conflict is equally nerve-wracking for the parent. Sounds of "this kid never listens to me" and "I can't take any more, I've had it" reverberate throughout the house. How often the parent's rage and punishment are totally out of line, disproportionate, to what the child did "wrong" (spilling some milk, not wanting to eat the green beans, not moving fast enough). The parent's reaction reflects its annoyance and frustration at having its MBH interfered with. Have you ever noticed that many parents yell at and berate the children they love in a way they would never speak to strangers? After all, you can disregard and escape strangers.

The answer, of course, lies somewhere in the parents remembering that MBH is a natural need of the child. To see MBH developing in a child should be a comforting sign to a parent. To squelch a child's development in this regard and/or to punish a child for being healthy, generates problems far beyond the spilled milk and is as unhealthy for the child and for the parent-child relationship as is imaginable.

Well, you may ask, should there not be some rules in the house so that the house can run smoothly? Certainly. Rules about not pulling your sister's hair, not going outside to play in the snow without shoes on. Rules about not interfering in another's MBH. (Believe it or not, this concept can be explained to even a very young child. "I know you want to be able to do what you want to do and I know that you understand that I, too, would like to be able to do what I want to do. And if we can find a way that both of us get what we want, wouldn't that be great?") And make the rules fair and reasonable to all, including the child.

But, otherwise, very few rules, if rules mean dictates. Children want to learn. They want to love and be loved. They want to be part of, and to enjoy the security of, a functioning family. It is the responsibility of the parents to teach their children why the "right" thing to do is indeed the right thing to do. In other words, even at very tender ages, children should be approached through their Minds. Parents should seek to persuade through reason as to the propriety of what they are asking, thus helping to promote reason as the guideline for the child's future action and lifestyle. And one way to resolve conflicts of MBH's between a parent and a child is to offer the child a choice ("Would you like to sit quietly in this room with me and read a book, or would you rather go into the other room and watch television?") This places the child in a position to make up its own Mind and to act out its own decisions.

Of course, spanking is out. It is a major MB breach (as well as, in my opinion, a form of child abuse). It seeks to convince a child of something by force exerted against its Body, rather than by reason addressed to its Mind. It seeks to train, rather than teach, a child...the way we appropriately deal with non-reasoning animals. Remember, too, that a child who is overly and unreasonably punished for admitting having done something wrong may likely not speak out, or may lie about matters, to avoid excessive punishment in the future. Wouldn't you?

Proper parenting is a time-consuming profession. It requires, on the part of the parents, education, understanding, discipline, patience, consistency and love. And all of them in super large doses!

Helping to develop an independent, functioning human being is one of the great opportunities of life.

CHAPTER 11

THE CRUELEST HOAX

From the time a child is old enough to understand and often long before that, society begins its assault on its next victim.

He is taught to conform to the rules, the mores, the standards of society, to get along, in exchange for acceptance and security, and this induces him to suppress his own thoughts, his own feelings, his own self. He befriends the unworthy, he agrees not to disagree, he is told not to stand out and he doesn't. He discovers, too late, that the security he seeks leaves him insecure within himself.

He is told not to "think that way," not to "say those things," not to "be like that," when that is the way he wishes to think, to speak, to be. In other words, he is told not to be himself, or herself, which is a contradiction, an impossibility.

He is told to gauge his success, to measure his worth, by the approval of others and he courts that approval at the cost of his own soul. He is taught not to be proud of his achievements, which means not to be proud of himself, which places happiness outside his reach.

He is told to do his duty to family, to country, to society, which means to act not in accordance with the judgments of his own Mind but with the judgments of others, which means to live without his Mind, which means to live a living death.

In school, he is taught the past but not the future, ancient history but not how to achieve his goals, how to get along with others but not how to know himself, the laws of the jungle but not the laws of logic. And the results are self-evident. Look around!

He is told that it is moral to sacrifice his life to others, and so he does, and he becomes yet another lamb on the altar of death.

He is told that life's rewards come in another life so he stops expecting them here on Earth. Many destroy themselves to escape the anguish of an unrewarding life.

He is told that money is the root of all evil but he wants some and so he feels evil, sinful, unworthy.

He is told not to judge others, that we are all the same, but he does judge, as he must, and he discovers we are not all the same and he feels bewildered and guilty.

He is taught to fear failure, to fear rejection, so he runs from the enriching challenges and involvements of life.

He is taught that ideas do not matter, that they are but mental games that have no important meaning in his life, and so they don't.

He is told there is no truth and he is relieved to hear it for he could not find it in any event. Truthlessness, he is told, has set him free.

He is told that being born into a society has automatically made him a signatory to a social contract that decrees what he must do to satisfy his obligations to society. He is advised that from time to time, society will define and clarify for him the duties he owes to society and the financial obligations he owes to other, less endowed, less industrious, members of society. He is told that failure to do such duties and to pay such financial obligations (via taxes and other assessments) is punishable by fine and/or imprisonment, in amounts and duration set from time to time by society.

He is advised not to question, criticize nor contest either society's authority under this social contract or his obligations hereunder under penalty of being labeled a radical, a rebel, an iconoclast, an idealist, a troublemaker, each of whom is punishable by social banishment.

He is promised that in return for his obedience and fulfillment of the terms of this social contract, he will be permitted to be an accepted member of society.

Now, of course, such a contract could have no legal efficacy, could it? After all, it was imposed upon you without your consent and if you do not agree with the terms of the contract, you are still forcefully bound by them. It is a contract that our courts would not enforce, would they?

But they do, every day, with respect to virtually every aspect of our lives. (Remember, the judges and prosecuting attorneys are members of society.) As someone who speaks out in favor of individualism and freedom, I am forever accosted by even well-intentioned people who remind me of my obligations under the social contract. Obligations now backed by the force of law. I have been granted a privilege, they say, to live in society and I must pay the price that society exacts. Of course, there is no limit as to what that price may be since society, and society alone, sets the terms of the social contract. My life, it appears, was mortgaged without my consent, from the start.

If I choose to obey, I become a pawn to be used in the "public interest." If I choose not to obey, I am punished. Clever! Either way, I am being coerced to live my life, to some extent, in accordance with the wishes of the Minds of others. A set of MB breaches imposed on me by my fellow citizens, my dear neighbors, my colleagues.

Society, my alleged benefactor, is, in fact, an assassin!

CHAPTER 12

BUT IS IT A CRIME?

Should prostitution be a crime? Should we legalize marijuana and other drugs? Should bigamy be a crime? What activities should a reasoned society label as criminal, and why?

The concept of MBH offers a sensible standard to use in determining whether a particular activity ought or ought not be deemed a crime. Any activity that inflicts an MB breach on another ought be a crime, since it is an attack on, and violates, the other person's natural state. Any activity that does not inflict such a breach ought not be considered a crime.

Steal someone's property? That is a crime under this standard since it interferes with the owner's right to deal with his or her property as he or she sees fit. Rape? Clearly a crime since it is the forceful asserting of one's Mind over the Body of another.

Prostitution? No MB breach and thus no crime if the parties are consenting adults. An adult engaging in prostitution with a minor is engaged in what is tantamount to an act of force against the minor (who is too young to make such a critical sexual decision) and that force is criminal.

A person smoking marijuana or taking hard drugs? No MB breach and no crime, since the person is doing what he or she chooses to do and is not inflicting an MB breach on another. A person who commits robbery while under the influence of drugs is committing a crime, but it is the robbery, and not the taking of drugs, that imposes the MB breach on another and is criminal.

A person selling such drugs to a minor is, as in the case of prostitution, engaging in an act tantamount to an act of force against the child (since the child is too young to make a reasoned decision about the use of drugs), and that is criminal.

There are those who would say that hard drugs are not good for you and that, accordingly, the Government has the right to restrict and punish its use. Notice how that places the Minds of others (those who pass the laws) in a priority position to the Mind of the one using the drugs. That is an MB breach. An adult person has the right to inhale or digest whatever he or she wishes and that right cannot properly be denied by the whims, wishes or dictates of others. What is wrong about taking hard drugs is that those drugs impair the capacity of the Mind to think and to do its decision-making job and the taking of them is, therefore, immoral. But, for reasons I have indicated, ought not be considered criminal.

Some people refer to the MBH concept as "freedom"...the right to live your life as you choose. Freedom permits harmony between your thoughts and your actions. Since that freedom can only be interfered with by an act of force, freedom is the right to live without the initiation of force, physical force, against you. (In this regard, fraud is a method of taking someone else's property, or time or affection, without consent, and is thus a taking through a variant of physical force.) Since each person has an equal right to be free, freedom is not a license to initiate force (or fraud) against anyone else.

There are those who argue for the concept of a restricted or partial freedom, granting society the right to limit an individual's freedom when the needs of society so "require." But the idea of a restricted or partial freedom is a contradiction, an impossibility, an oxymoron. Either you are, or you are not, free. Like the slave who remains a slave even if he is given a few hours off by his master, so you and I, if even for one moment of one day we are subject to the dictates of anyone else, then we are not free in any proper use of that term. We are slaves. (Which is the state of affairs Mr. Patrick Henry said he could not live with. It is the state of affairs that no one can live with.)

Those who believe in restricted freedom often ask: What would our society be like if everyone were free to do as he or she wished?

I am reminded of the woman who lived in Hungary and who came to visit her son, a friend of mine, in New York City. Walking up and down Fifth Avenue, she was fascinated by life in the city. "There are stores of every type, everything you need and more is available to you, things seem to work so well," she said. "How can that be? How does that work out if everyone is free to do what he or she wishes to do?" The woman, you see, had come from a communist-dominated country with no freedom and total regulation and had been told since early age that society had to be organized if it were to function well. And that is what she believed.

The truth, of course, is the reverse. Society works best when it is a free society. Freedom works! It is the natural state of affairs for man and the best environment in which humans can function. It is slavery that doesn't work.

Should bigamy be a crime? If all parties consent to it (as is sometimes the case), then it ought not be considered a crime since there is no act of force against another. If, however, one of the parties is not aware of the bigamy being committed (say, a woman is enticed to "marry" a man who is already married and who conceals that critical fact from her), then that ought be labeled a crime...it entails the fraudulent taking of another's property (sexual intimacy, love, labor, money, etc.) without the other person's consent to the true facts.

Should avoidance of the military draft be a crime? No. What more devastating assault on MBH can there be than to require someone to risk his (or her) life against his (or her) will? To suggest that there may be national reasons and needs that require the imposition of the military draft, to curtail an individual's freedom, is to reawaken the specter of the concept of duty and all of its errors previously noted. There can be no national reasons to deny freedom...that is, deny man's natural state.

That it is the Government, the agency set up to protect our need for and right to MBH, that seeks to impose this devastating MB breach on its citizens, is doubly onerous. If the Government needs to beef up its military force, it must do so by persuasion. It must go to the citizenry and attempt to convince them that the war it wishes to engage in is an appropriate one and that its citizens ought volunteer to serve. This places a burden on the Government and one it ought to bear. It must convince the citizenry of the appropriateness of the battles it wishes to engage in. One favorable consequence of this is that the Government may have difficulty recruiting soldiers to fight in conflicts in which the Government ought not be engaged in the first place. Think of American history and the number of draftees who died in such type wars.

Should the avoidance of income taxes be a crime? No, since all taxes represent an unwarranted and immoral taking of money, the imposition of MB breaches on taxpayers, who have the right to spend or otherwise dispose of their money as they, and they alone, see fit.

Well, you might ask, how will the Government raise the money it needs to run the country, without taxes? Whatever the answer to that question (lotteries, voluntary contributions, fees for services provided, etc.), it must not include the denial of the nature of human beings and the denial of freedom. If the Government is intended to serve human lives, how can it properly include procedures that destroy those lives?

So, my formulation:

    Imposition of MB Breach on Another = Crime.

People may differ on its application to specific circumstances, but they ought not differ on the equation itself.

CHAPTER 13

THE DEFENSE

I said earlier that we have not only not been taught to strive for MBH, but that we have been consistently taught and encouraged by virtually every segment of our society to accept MB breaches. I have given a number of examples to prove that point. Now I wish to make certain recommendations as to how this continuing assault on MBH can be defeated.

PARENTS: Almost always, parents are the first and primary influence in our lives. It is from watching them and how they live their lives that we often learn what we will believe to be are the proper principles to live by. If our parents spank us, we may learn that force is an appropriate way to resolve problems. And by implication, we learn that it is acceptable to bypass the Mind, to coerce others to do our bidding when they don't wish to do it.

If we hear our parents tell us that we should always obey the law, but then see them speeding on the highway, we may come to believe that there are, indeed, two different standards to apply: one for thinking and one for acting. This is Plato's deadly two-world philosophy and the prime source of the clashes referred to previously. Again, what we learn by implication is that action (the Body) need not follow thought (the Mind), and that integrity between Mind and Body is not necessarily a virtue.

When parents tell us that it is our duty to respect them, regardless of their behavior, when they tell us to do something because "I told you to do it, that's why," when they tell us that it is important for us to get along with others even when we do not comprehend a reason to do so, they are promoting MB breaches that will ultimately take their toll on our lives and our chances for happiness.

Many parents seek to inculcate in their children's Minds the idea that it is important to like and be friendly with all members of the family (including aunts, uncles, cousins, and the like), with other students in their classes, with neighbors and with just about everyone else they come in contact with, even when such people have not, by their behavior, earned such friendship and such treatment. The underlying message? Your Mind and your judgments do not matter. And further, such a "be nice to everybody" attitude attacks the idea of justice...that people ought be treated for who and what they are, rather than that they all be treated the same regardless of their character, their virtues, or lack thereof.

Most parents, no doubt, are well intentioned and certainly have the interests of their children at heart. But since they themselves have been taught the wrong things, given the wrong messages, it is not surprising (is it?), that they pass the same wrong ideas along to their children.

What is surprising is that most of us undertake the critical job of parenting without the slightest bit of study. Most of us know little about parenting and figure (if we think about it at all) that somehow we will do the right things because "we've had a good upbringing, we are pretty smart and we mean well." Many people believe that good parenting comes naturally...it doesn't...and discover much too late that maybe they didn't do the best at this critical job and discover, too, the extent of the damage they have caused their progeny.

Think about it. We take courses to learn to type, how to fix cars, how to make clay pots. But few of us take any classes on how to raise children, perhaps the first or second most important job we will ever have. We undertake responsibility for human life without understanding what human life needs and how human life functions. Under the banner of good intentions, we assault the lives of those most dear to us, those who trust us to do what is best for them, those who cannot defend themselves.

What can and should parents do?

1. During the period of pregnancy (if not before), both parents should study the nature of the human being they are bringing into this world...both physical and mental (including the need for MBH)...so that they will be in a position to help it flourish and be happy. They should seek out books, attend lectures and study groups that explicitly or implicitly support the concept of MBH.

2. Teach the child at a very young age, and on its own terms, the value and pleasure of MBH.

3. Encourage the child to think for itself and refrain from imposing their will on the child except in those circumstances involving danger or pain to the child or to others, and then always to remember to give reasons for their decisions.

4. Monitor what is being taught the child in school, become active in PTA groups, speak out against principles and ideas which promote MBH breaches.

5. Show by example that ideas are important and that living in accordance with proper principles is noble and virtuous.

The result of this will likely be healthy children passing along healthy principles to their children, who pass along healthy principles to their children, and so on.

TEACHERS: Second only to the influence of parents is the effect which early grade teachers have on the child's mental development. Teachers should do the following:

1. Remember that the function of education is to help a child develop its cognitive faculty...the ability to reason, to solve problems, to make decisions. The child's Mind is the motor that will drive the child's life. Enhancing the Mind's abilities and the process by which it works will enrich that life more than anything else the teacher may do. Memorized knowledge has relatively minimal importance, as does the grading of it.

2. Teach logical thinking, objective thinking, to even young children so that they develop the proper mental methods to employ throughout every phase of their lives. Identify for children the most common logical flaws so that they may avoid making them, and so that they will be alert to them when those flaws are made to them.

3. Teach the role and mechanics of the Mind so that children will have a good reason not to do those things that

limit the Mind's ability to perform its function (e.g., taking hard drugs).

4. Eliminate the grading of a child's ability to get along with others and monitor instead the child's ability to think for itself and to make decisions on its own.

5. Illustrate the joy of independent thinking.

6. Colleges, universities and adult education centers should offer parenting courses...taught by teachers who themselves understand the significance of MBH and the role it plays in a child's life. These courses should include a whole range of issues relative to raising a healthy child, including nutrition, discipline, independent thinking, outspokenness, and so on.

PHYSICIANS: Living in accordance with your nature stimulates good health, mental and physical. I have indicated that there are adverse effects to not living an MBH existence, including frustration, despair, depression and more. Just as a physician ought advise parents about steps to take to avoid physical illness, rather than simply treating illness after it occurs, so, too, ought the physician advise parents about the notion of MBH, the potential physiological damage if it is not adhered to, and the damage to the child's mental health and maturation that will likely occur if MBH is not fostered.

Physicians must also know the medical aspects of MBH: that mental strains and pressures and states of mind can have physical effects, and that physical illnesses, diseases and malfunctions can affect the health and functioning of the Mind.

GOVERNMENT: Politicians and other government officials must remember that the government is a wielder of force, that it has the power to enforce its laws by the imposition of penalties and imprisonment. They must be certain that the laws that they impose do not violate MBH.

I have written about this matter earlier with regard to crimes. But the government must be limited even in non-criminal matters, whenever they seek to interfere with or limit the right of an individual to live by the judgments of his or her own Mind.

For example, the government ought not impose special tariffs on goods coming in from other countries (in an attempt to have Americans buy American). It is an aspect of freedom and free choice that an individual not be penalized for buying from whomever or wherever he or she wishes to buy (unless the purchase be from an enemy of our country that threatens to deny us our freedom).

Minimum wage laws that limit the right of adults to be paid for labor below a government-established minimum, even when the adult agrees to such wages, are an attack on MBH.

Anti-trust laws, which limit how much of a market someone may control, how successful someone may be, violate MBH and should not be imposed.

The list goes on and on. What is important is for the government to realize that inflicting MB breaches is doubly deadly: it is, per se, a violation of freedom and it strengthens the idea that such violations are appropriate.

Ultimately, the assault on MBH is an attack on ideas as such ("Ideas don't matter, do whatever you wish or do what others wish"). And since ideas move man, it is an attack on man. The defense against the assault must be constant, strident and courageous.

A few years ago, I wrote this:

> "If man wishes to enjoy life to the fullest, he must choose to be himself, or herself, in the deepest meaning of that expression,
>
> He must think for himself, live for his own happiness, act in his own rational self-interest,
>
> He must keep his mind and his body unshackled from the will of others,
>
> He must revel in the value of his own being,
>
> He must first come to know that he is sovereign."

CHAPTER 14

WHAT IS SUCCESS?

The Random House dictionary defines success this way:

"(T)he favorable or prosperous termination of attempts or endeavors, the attainment of wealth, position, honors, or the like, a successful performance or achievement (as in 'the play was an instant success') and a thing or a person that is successful."

Now, those are the common uses of the word "success" and you will notice that the definitions deal with two different types of success: the obtaining of something that you wish (what I call "short-term" success: the obtaining of an isolated or a short-term goal) and being a successful person, having a successful life (what I call "long-term" success).

(The idea that "the play was an instant success" does not make much sense to me, as you will see. I think of that more as the author, the producer, the director, the actors, were successful in presenting a play that was well-received by the public...and so I drop "the play was successful" into the category of short-term success.)

Let's take a look first at short-term success, the obtaining of something that you wish or desire in the short-term. The getting of something. You want something, you get it, you are successful. You want a college degree, you get it, you are successful. You want someone to marry you, he or she does, you are successful.

There are two important questions to think about in regard to short-term success:

> Does it matter what it is that you want?

> Does it matter how you go about getting it?

Is it appropriate to use the word "success" to refer to the getting of something that a rational human shouldn't want to get? Either because it is anti-life, or it is obtained through immorality or criminality?

For example: I need and want a job. I see an advertisement in the newspaper that indicates that a company is looking for someone who majored in journalism. I didn't major in journalism, but I am an OK writer, so I set up an appointment for an interview. When I get there, I lie to the company and tell them, "Yes, I majored in journalism," and I get the job.

May I appropriately say that I was successful in landing the job? Or is that an immoral way to get a job that ought not, and cannot rationally, be thought of as a success?

Or, I am a hit man for the underworld. I am ordered to go out and kill someone, someone who doesn't want to pay protection money to the family I belong to. I plan the murder very carefully, track my victim, learn his every move, his habits, and so on. And then I do it, I murder the guy and, thanks to my careful planning, I don't get caught. May I appropriately say that I was successful in doing my job, my dirty deed? Can the word "success" be properly tied to murder, to the doing of an evil act?

Or, I want to fail. Failure validates and reinforces my malevolent sense of life. So, I fail. May I appropriately say, "I was successful in achieving failure"? After all, if I was successful, then I didn't fail. Which is what I wanted to do. Yet the only way to fail at achieving failure is to succeed. Or can I fail and succeed at the same time?

Successful failure is an oxymoron, a contradiction, which means it is axiomatically impossible and thus irrational to a rational human being. Failure in achieving values is anti-life and the obtaining of anti-life goals ought not, and cannot rationally, be thought of as success, which is the obtaining of pro-life goals.

And getting a job through deception is dishonest, which is immoral, which is irrational to a rational human being. (And if you get a job through deception, was it *you* that got the job? No, it wasn't. Since you made up your supposed credentials, it wasn't *you* that applied and got the job. And soon you and your made-up friend will be fired, when your lie is uncovered or your inadequacies revealed.)

There are no values, after all, in nonreality, and that is where lies place you. Things, goals, values, exist only in reality. Stepping outside of reality to get them is to find yourself in the realm of nonthings, nongoals, nonvalues. Because success connotes the obtaining of a value, it ought never be associated with anti-life immorality or criminality.

In other words, the word "success" must be considered in light of who is being successful and if that is a human being, then it must be gauged in the context of what values and goals and actions are rational to a human being. And rationality hinges on the nature of man, including MBH.

To a rat, sneaking into your home and invading your food supply and getting out of the house without being caught is a successful act. To a human being, doing the same thing, it is not.

We need a word to describe what happens when one obtains something irrational or obtains something irrationally. And the word "got" seems perfect. Like, "I had to lie to get the job, of course. But I got it." Or, "The family wanted me to get that son of a gun and I got him right between the eyes." Gotcha! Got away with it. Not "success," just, "got."

Relative to a rational animal, "success" connotes rational values rationally obtained.

Another reason why murdering someone cannot properly be thought of as a success is because the doing of it comes attached with many painful strings. Imagine the murder. It comes with the following baggage:

* The denial of the right to life as a principle, both for the victim and the murderer (and what greater loss can the murderer experience, other than his life, than the loss of the right to life, the value of knowing that one is alive and that one has the right to live free and unbothered).

* The stress that comes from the constant and continuous fear of being caught, of being turned in by confederates, of being imprisoned for years and years and years.

* The making of truth and reality into an enemy (after all, if the truth be known, the murderer will be punished, incarcerated or put to death).

* The inability to trust others, who may also be murderers.

* The loss of self-esteem that comes from knowing that you are not good enough to succeed in life in a rational, peaceful, honorable way.

And on and on. The murdering of someone comes with substantial baggage, negative baggage, which colors the act from success (had it been a moral act) to dismal failure.

And the same holds true for the improper getting of a job: the loss of self-esteem that comes from knowing that you are not good enough to get this job, the constant fear that your lie will be found out, the constant lying and the deception you must practice to cover for your original lie, the absurdity you feel when you punish your children for lying to you, and on and on. And the same general pattern holds true with regard to all other immoral, irrational acts. They are not success stories; they are dismal, painful, failure stories.

And so, when you see someone who is engaging in some evil or immoral act, or pursuing some evil or immoral goal, consider the totality of the act: the act itself and all of its consequences. To evaluate an act without evaluating its consequences is to be myopic, intellectually shortsighted.

Imagine, if you would, that you have just picked up a lit stick of dynamite. Someone yells, "Throw it as far away from you as you can." So you do. You toss the lit stick of dynamite 30 feet into the air directly over your head. That is as far as you can throw it. Would you describe that as a successful act? Only if you can separate the cause from the effect and deny the law of gravity. That is, only if you can deny the consequences of the act, deny the totality of what you have just done.

Cause and effect ought not properly be divided into two separate, distinct things...one possibly a success and one possibly a failure. A successful act with failing consequences is a contradiction. A successful act with failing consequences is a failing act. To see cause without seeing effect is to deny the nature of reality. The effects are properly linked and considered together with the cause because that is what happens...when you implement the cause, you implement the effects. They go hand-in-hand. They are to all intents and purposes, one...and they must be judged that way.

Long-term success is different from short-term success in a number of important ways. First, its *scope*. A successful life encompasses your total being. It is not merely the obtaining of a specific rational value in a rational way. It does not apply to isolated events and goals in your life, but to your entire life, your psyche, your sense of the world and your sense of self. As such, long-term success must be viewed and thought of in a different way. Success over the span of one's life is not simply the sum of its successful parts. To think it must be is to commit the fallacy of composition: believing that what is true of the parts is necessarily true of the whole.

Second, success in life, a successful life, entails a *goal* that is not, and cannot directly be, found in the short-term. It is the goal of happiness. All human action ultimately leads toward or away from happiness. You want a job in order to express yourself, you wish to express yourself because it will help make you happy. You want to close a particular deal because it will make you a lot of money, you want the money because it will enable you to buy things, you want to buy things because they will help make you happy. All rational goals and actions put you on the path toward happiness.

Happiness is a psychological and emotional state that entails a long term of activity. It cannot be obtained in the short run. It is a long-term goal requiring long-term effort.

And third, because of reasons one and two, success or failure in life is a high stakes affair...you have spent a long-term to attain it or not, it is an *all or nothing* affair (either you are or you are not happy)...and if you fail, there may be no second chances.

For all of these reasons, it is imperative that we not predicate success on the actions of others. In dealing with short-term goals, which often entail the involvement of others, basing your success in part on their actions is not usually critical. There will, in all likelihood, be other opportunities to achieve the same goals, maybe even better ones.

But in regard to success in the long-term, there may be no other opportunities. To place this one, critical, all-consuming, reward of happiness, lifetime happiness, in the hands of others, would be world-class folly. It would attack the whole concept of individualism and independence that is inherent in MBH. To base success on the thoughts or actions of others would make you a dependent being, placing the Minds of others in a preemptive position relative to your own Mind in regard to this critical issue of life success.

How, then, is long-term success to be determined? This way. If you, as a human being, have done substantially everything that you ought to do, as determined by your nature as a human being, to enrich and nourish your life, then you are successful. What more could be asked of you? If you exert your maximum potential effort, or close to it, then you are successful, regardless of how others respond to you...that is, regardless of how many cars you sell, how high on the corporate ladder you reach, how much money you acquire, etc. The folly, the shortsightedness, the biases of others in no way diminish the quality of your life's achievements nor your entitlement to call your life a success.

We are, each of us, sovereign beings. We have been given the greatest gift of all...life...and we have every reason to judge our lives by what we make of this gift, what we make of our lives: Ourselves. That is our greatest challenge, and it ought to be our crowning achievement if we meet that challenge successfully. It ought be the source of our greatest pride, what we ought to be most happy about.

How do you make the most of yourself? What does "the most of yourself" mean? How do you know if you are making the most of yourself if the way people respond to you is not the criterion?

The measurement is reality, including the reality of your nature as a human being, which includes the reality of the value of MBH.

In the first chapter of "The Fountainhead" by Ayn Rand, Howard Roark, a young college student, is being expelled from architecture school because he refuses to design buildings in the traditional way and wishes to design them in his own style. He tells the Dean of the school that modern materials permit new designs and that the form of the building should reflect its function.

"Do you mean to tell me," begrudgingly bellows the Dean, "that you're thinking seriously of building that way, when and if you are an architect?"

"Yes," says Roark.

"My dear fellow," says the Dean, "who will let you?"

"That's not the point," says Roark. "The point is, who will stop me?"

That is MBH in action. A person's own Mind not needing the acquiescence, the permission, the direction, the approval, of others. A shining example of conviction, determination, courage, individualism, integrity. Was that a successful meeting for Roark, who is expelled from school? You bet it was!

Consistently live MBH, in the full meaning of that term, and make moral choices, and you are a success in life.

I have previously indicated and discussed in detail the fact that there are two aspects to MBH: first, that the Mind and the Body act in harmony with their nature, and, second, that they act in harmony with each other.

The Mind is a volitional consciousness...that is, you must choose to put it to work.

MBH kicks in, or not, from the first moment each day when you wake up and throw your legs over the side of the bed. Do you choose to jump start your Mind or not? To be in focus or not? And what do you choose to be in focus about? Something meaningful, important in and to your life, or something trivial, irrelevant, banal? Are there significant parts of the day when you are not in focus, when you are a mere spectator of life rather than an active participant in it? If so, MBH is not an active, viable element in your life.

What do you eat for breakfast? Something nourishing, or some sugared cereal with little nutritional value? What type of job will you go to? A job that challenges the best that is within you, that challenges you to do and be your best, or a run of the mill job, a "can do this in my sleep job," working with people that you are not particularly interested in, who have little to offer you, whose favorite and repeated saying is, "Thank God it's Friday."

I remember that one time I asked a Sister in a church how long it had been since she had taken a vacation. "Vacation?" she asked. "Why would I want to take a vacation? There is nothing in the world I would rather do than work constantly for the church and for God."

I am not suggesting by any means that to be a card-carrying member of the MBH club, you must feel that way about your job ...there are values other than work, though work is at or near the top of the list...but something close to the Sister's dedication and connection to her work would be appropriate.

Have you ever made a list of your friends and asked yourself why you are friendly with each of them, and did you have rational reasons for all of the friendships? Or are there people with whom you are friends because all you can say of them is, "I guess I've known them a long time."

Does fear still play an important part in your decisions? Fear of failure, fear of success, fear of having your image and your reputation tarnished? And when you are confronted with feelings of fear, do you succumb, or do you gather more data, consider alternative options, etc.? Are your fears rational, and if they aren't, do you dismiss them on the basis of their irrationality?

How many people really know you? And is that because you find endless reasons not to tell them what you really think, how you really feel, who you really are? Do you constantly keep things to yourself because you don't want to hurt other people, do you repeatedly compromise your desire to be outspoken because you believe that it's easier to do that than to take the consequences of antagonizing others?

Can you argue persuasively why you live where you live? Of all the places in the country, in the world, why do you live where you live? Did you make a choice about that, or did it just come to be?

Are you satisfied that your Mind thinks about all of the important decisions in your life, so that you can honestly say that you are the primary cause of virtually all of the events in your life...or do you let things happen to you because you're tired of fighting, tired of expending the effort it takes to live independently?

Do you carpe diem...seize the day? Is each day important to you in terms of productivity, in terms of enjoying the physicalities of the world, of moving ever closer to (or of reinforcing) happiness? Are your senses open and receiving...or do you often look without seeing, listen without hearing, taste without savoring?

When I was a child of ten or so, my father would ask me each night, when I went to bed, "What one thing do you know now that you did not know this morning?" If you asked yourself that question each evening, how often would you answer, "Nothing"? If the question were, "What one thing did you do today that you never did before?"...or, if the question were, "What one thought did you have today that you never had before?"...what would your answers be?

And let's not forget the Body. If the Body is to do what it is meant to do, to carry out the directions of the Mind, then the Body must be in shape to do it. Thus, the nourishing and nurturing of the Body is vital to MBH.

MBH is a driving energy force, once you adopt it as your way of life, that can lift you out of the doldrums, that lights the way to achievement, happiness and success, that keeps you on track as a human being, that helps to bring out the best that is within you, that can see you through the difficult times. MBH is a shield to ward off irrational pressures...it will help you stay guilt-free...it will give you clarity of vision, peace of mind...and it can do all of this because it unites you with your nature, intellectually, physically, emotionally.

To understand MBH and to adopt adherence to it as a critical element of your philosophy and to live by its tenets on a daily basis...moment-to-moment daily basis...to gain control over your life...that is an inordinate achievement and success. What happens thereafter, happens...and nothing that happens thereafter can diminish, stain or deny that success.

The human Mind is a tool of inordinate capability. I don't know whether we generally use only 5% of the Mind's capacity, or 10%, or whatever. What I do know is that there always seems to be more to use. What I do know is that a human Mind that stays within itself, that only does things that it has done before, gets bored and begins to automatize its functions and to shut down. The human Mind has the capacity, robotlike, to repeat mundane activities with a minimum of thoughtful activity. Put another way, a human Mind needs to be pushed out into new regions if it is to stay on the track of its potentiality and get ever closer to its maximum output...and one important and significant way to do that is through creativity.

I know of no human mental activity that feels as rewarding, as fulfilling, as to be creative in whatever field you may choose to be creative in. Write a new song, develop a new piece of software, create a new recipe, design a new logo, and on and on. Creativity challenges the human Mind and rewards the human Mind with a great sense of efficacy and pride and of individuality. "I did it. I did it. Wow!" To be an adherent of MBH is to push out the limits of your knowledge, your production...to visualize and then to actualize...to be as much as you can be, and always more than you are.

It takes all of that and more to earn the right to call yourself an MBH adherent. Must you be focused all the time, productive all the time? No. There is certainly a value to rest and recuperation and relaxation...and there will certainly be times when you simply do not feel very energetic, very creative, very anything other than lazy. We are, after all, human...and remember that thing about the *volitional* consciousness. But if that is the pattern of your life, if that mental shutdown occurs too often (and no, I don't know exactly how many hours per day or per week qualifies for mental shutdown), then it would be an anti-MBH thing to do.

We must be careful not to make MBH part of a Mind Body breach. MBH is part of a philosophy to live by...and it requires your mental understanding and conviction as well as your physical action. That is, to call yourself an MBH aficionado, you must do more than adopt MBH as part of your philosophy; you must live it, consistently and proudly, over a period of time.

I am an individual and I ought be judged, praised or condemned, by what I and I alone do and by who I and I alone am...that is, by what I and I alone have made of myself.

What makes for a successful marriage? One thing is for sure, and that is that longevity is no more a measurement of a successful marriage than tenure is a measure of a good teacher. "Been married thirty years," people say, as if that means something other than they've been married thirty years, which in my mind is no more worth a blue ribbon than to say, "Haven't been married thirty years."

There are all sorts of reasons that can work toward making for a happy marriage. Like management of life. Today it takes a lot of effort just to manage your life...shopping and cleaning and paying bills and keeping records and mowing the lawn and sending out Christmas cards and all sorts of things...and husbands and wives can share those chores. Or, a husband or wife can marry someone who is good at all those types of things. Does that make for a successful marriage? No, not really...certainly not by itself. All of those things can be done by maids and accountants and secretaries. But they can be a factor to a happy marriage, to some minimum extent.

There is ministering...ministering to each other in times of physical and emotional need, support, encouragement, shoulder to lean on...enriching the other person's life. Does that make for a successful marriage? Again, all of those things can be done by friends and physicians and counselors. They are not exclusive to marriage...but they can help, certainly.

There is parenting. I've spoken about that. There is sharing: the sharing of life and life's pleasures. Even an independent-minded individualist can recognize the additional benefits that may come from sharing life's pleasures.

There is another factor that can be of enormous influence on whether the marriage is successful...and it is what I refer to as The Search for Objective Identity.

Man lives within his Mind within reality. He, or she, sees the world from the confines of his or her Mind. He looks out at the world to see what is "out there." What he does not see "out there" is himself, or herself.

Man can introspect, and look inward...but unless he has attained objective perfection, that introspection can be clouded with fears, with wishes and fancies, with misguided self-evaluations, with psychological colorations that can distort what is being seen. It is true that introspection can be of great value, if...if...the picture and the vision are clear.

It is interesting that most of us never even see our true physicality. Mirrors don't do it. The images we see in the mirror are not us; they are mirror images of us. Ever notice that when people see themselves on VCR tapes or on movie film, they invariably say, "I didn't think I look like that. Do I really look like that? I look different."

When I studied voice in New York, I asked my teacher whether I hear myself the way I actually sound. No you don't, he told me...and he told me the technical reasons for that, which I have forgotten...but I do remember him saying that if I wanted to hear what I actually sound like to others, I should face into the corner of a room, and speak. That is the way to hear how you actually sound, or as close to it as you can get. So, most of us probably don't even know what we sound like!

Do you often hear people who are arguing saying things like, "But I am not like that. I'm exactly the reverse. What do you mean I'm not sensitive? I'm very sensitive. What do you mean I don't listen to what you have to say? I always listen to what you have to say. What do you mean I never agree with you? I always agree with you," and so on.

Man's thirst for knowledge quite naturally includes, perhaps above all, his thirst for knowledge about himself. "Who am I?"..."What am I?"..."What do I project?"...these are critical questions, the answers to which man must know if he is to know how to get from here to there, if he is to learn from things that have happened to him, if he is to understand and appreciate himself, to love himself. There is a natural and pervasive need to "know thyself," despite society's constant admonitions not to make yourself the center of your life, not to pay too much attention to yourself, not to take yourself too seriously. I can imagine nothing more important for a person to know, than to know himself or herself. Pluses and minuses.

And here is where a spouse can be of inordinate value. Seeing you on a daily basis in the most intimate of relationships and circumstances, both physically and emotionally naked, as it were, your spouse can reflect back the objective identity you so desperately need. This is one of the reasons why it is so important to be honest in the marriage relationship...so that the spouse gets to see and hear and feel the true nature of his or her mate. That will aid in enhancing the value of the identity feedback that your spouse can give you. And if you have, hopefully, chosen a mate whose judgments and perspectives and sense of life you value, then the feedback comes to you together with an overall acceptance of who you are, and a desire to help you know yourself and to succeed in all you do.

To your spouse, you are part of the "out there," you are a visible part of your spouse's reality, you are tangible.

When you hear a husband, or a wife, say, "My spouse doesn't know me, doesn't understand me," you are hearing of a marriage that does not have its most vital underpinning, its most critical foundation... and a marriage that is not serving one of the unique purposes it has the capacity to serve.

And, of course, there is reciprocity. You mirroring back the objective identity of your spouse. When we are cut off from our spouse, whether by divorce or death, we are cut off, temporarily, from our ourselves, our mirror...and even though we may find new companionship, there is still that pressing need that needs to be filled.

Can someone other than a spouse satisfy our search for objective identity? Yes, possibly, to some extent...but not to the full scope that a spouse can. Because of the totality of the time spent with the spouse, the diversity of shared experiences and confidences, the sexual relations and what they reveal, I believe the spouse stands unique.

Management, ministration, parenting, sharing and mirroring all feed the happy successful marriage if done in a constructive, supportive, benevolent way.

I want to close this chapter by quoting another few lines by my personal hero, Howard Roark, in "The Fountainhead." It captures for me the essence of everything I believe about success:

"(Man's) moral law is never to place his prime goal within the persons of others."

"Independence is the only gauge of human virtue and value. What a man is and makes of himself; not what he has or hasn't done for others. There is no substitute for personal dignity. There is no standard of personal dignity except independence."

And there is no more appropriate standard of independence open to man than a strict and consistent loyalty to the concept of Mind Body Harmony in all of its meanings, ramifications, and applications, and a living of that harmony in a vital, uncompromised, way.

THE BIRTH OF RUPERT LYLE

A SHORT STORY

On Tuesday, the 23rd of September, at precisely 8:20 A.M., while walking from the train station to his office in midtown New York City, Rupert Lyle decided to be himself.

He admitted to himself that for most of his thirty-eight years he had said things he didn't mean and meant to say things he never did. He had lied to others and to himself. He had often done things without a goal in mind and he had many goals for which he had done nothing. He had rarely reached the happiness he knew was in him to attain, though he didn't know why. He felt he had a specific potential though he didn't know quite what it was. He knew he was special, but in what way?

He decided that from that moment on he would never think of himself as being anything but exactly what he was, he would never think of others as being anything but exactly what they were, he would never say a word that wasn't exactly what he thought, he would never again concern himself with anything but what was real. He decided to unravel the maze of his life, to enjoy life to the fullest, to be himself in the deepest meaning of that expression, to think for himself, to live for his own happiness. In other words, he decided to come alive.

"Good morning, Mr. Lyle, how are you?"

"Happy to be alive and free."
"I beg your pardon, Mr. Lyle?"

"Do you?"

"Do I what?"

"Beg my pardon."

"Huh?"

Rupert Lyle closed the door to his office and sat down at his desk. He did feel free, he thought. More: he felt without fear. What was there to be afraid of? He was what he was, nothing more, nothing less. He was Rupert Lyle. At any one moment in time there was a maximum to what he could do, he thought, and nothing more.

His responsibility to himself, he knew, was to reach for that maximum. It would be irresponsible of him, he thought, to accept a standard less than that maximum, or to bemoan the fact that he couldn't do more. It would take effort, constant effort, to be in touch with himself and the world out there. Everything in his life from now on would be defined, precise, meaningful. He would no longer accept the meek, the mediocre, the half-truth, as a standard of human conduct. He felt free of those chains that bound him to the mundane; he felt free to express and to succeed. And to fail. And to be happy.

Rupert took out a yellow pad of paper with red lines on it and wrote "GOALS" at the top of the top sheet. Underneath that, he made a list of the goals in his life. He crossed out some goals, added some, moved some higher or lower on the list. It took some effort, a willingness to confess the truth about himself to himself, but it was easier than he thought it would be. It was, surprisingly, fun. He smiled, noticing that that was one of his goals.

Finally, his list was complete, at least for then. Taking a fresh piece of paper, he started to write "GOALS" at the top of the page, but then wrote "ME" instead. He then listed, one under the other, the goals he had decided for himself, the ways in which he wished to live his life.

The list looked like this:

ME

To deal with things the way they are
To think independently
To be creative
To have integrity
To be free
To express the whole truth
To reach for the sublime
To be purposeful
To be fair
To have fun
To live an exciting life

At first, he wondered what he would do if ever there was a conflict between two goals and he had to make a choice between them. What standard would he use to make that choice? Did any goals have priority over the others?

But then something became clear to him. There was no real priority of importance to his goals. They were all equally important, equally critical to his life. To his happiness. They were, he realized, interrelated; each one, to some extent, intertwined with the others. There would never, could never, be a conflict between them. Rupert smiled again.

"Mr. Lyle," said the voice on the telephone intercom, "the President on line 2."

"Yes, Mr. Durney."

"Rupert, John McClintock is coming here tomorrow afternoon and I want you to meet with him. It's about the equipment for his new Boeings. Tell him the work is in process and will be ready in three weeks."

"Is it, sir?"

"Is it what?"

"In process. And will it be ready in three weeks?"

"No, dammit, it's not and it won't be for another two months, but tell McClintock it will be ready in three weeks."

Rupert glanced at his list of goals. "I can't do that, sir."

"Can't do what?"

"Lie, sir."

The voice screamed at him over the telephone. "What the hell are you talking about, Lyle?"

"I can't lie, sir. I'll have to tell McClintock the truth."

"Dammit, Lyle, what's wrong with you. McClintock won't accept the truth."

"What else is there to accept, sir?"

"What?"

"What else is there to accept in this world but the truth?"

"But this is business, Lyle."

"What kind of business?"

"Lyle, you're exasperating me and I have no time to talk with you. Do whatever you want to do, but let me tell you one thing. If we lose the McClintock order, you're fired."

"I know, sir."

"Did you hear me, Lyle?"

"I did, sir."

"Call me after the meeting," said Durney, and hung up.

"Thank you, Mr. Durney," said Rupert into the empty telephone, and hung up.

Rupert smiled. "Dammit," he screamed, "it's easy. It's easy." His voice was loud and resonant.

The door to his office opened and Rupert's secretary spoke to him from the doorway.

"I couldn't help hearing you, Mr. Lyle. What's easy?"

"Me."

"I beg your pardon, sir?"

"Me, me, me. It's easy to be me. Do you understand? It's easy to be me."

"I beg your pardon, sir?"

"I want to be alone."

"Yes, sir." Rupert's secretary closed the door, looking quizzically over her shoulder.

Rupert stood up and reached his hands toward the ceiling. Then he slapped his thigh.

"It's easy, damn it, it's so damn easy." He folded the yellow sheet with "ME" at the top and put it inside his wallet.

He felt as he thought a stage actor must feel the moment the curtain is raised, when he faces the audience and the play begins. All his life, Rupert had felt some thin curtain between him and his life, knowing what was waiting out there, but not quite being able to see it, to reach it. He had always felt the expectation and anxiety the actor must feel. Now, finally, the stage lights were turned up, the curtain raised, and he was "on." He could feel his pulse quicken, his blood flowing to every corner of his being, and his mind racing along confidently on a clear, precise course. He felt exhilarated, the most exhilarated he had ever felt in his life. "I am the author of my play," Rupert thought to himself, "the star of my life."

On the train going home that night, Rupert Lyle felt reborn. He noticed things he had never noticed before. He noticed that the lights in the train, just above the windows, were covered by glass in the shape of 1920 gaslights. He questioned how they were being fed electricity, until he saw a thin wire running along the top of each window frame, down its side to the baseboard and then running along the baseboard to the rear of the train's car. Probably a major outlet in one of those closed compartments at the back of each car, he thought, connected somehow to the train's engine. He wondered how the electricity was passed from one car to the next, and made a mental note to check the connections between the cars when he left the train.

He felt alive. He noticed colors, and even textures, around him. People in the train were three-dimensional, he noticed, and did not have their usual flat cardboard quality. He could smell autumn in the air. He thought he could feel the pulse beat in his fingertips. His mind seemed clear and only partially filled...waiting, it seemed, to be filled with...what?, he wondered...facts, judgments, pleasures, maybe a new goal or two.

Rupert was excited; he couldn't wait to fill his mind with life's bounties. What a joy, he thought, just to be alive. Strike the "just," he thought to himself. What an incredible joy to be alive!

The train stopped. Across the tracks was a small grassy area and Rupert could see a young man pushing a wind blower about the size of a grass cutter. By walking in smaller and smaller circles around the small park, the young man blew the thousands of fallen leaves, slowly but surely, into a pile in the center of the park. Rupert could see a small truck nearby, a long vacuum-type hose extending from its side, ready to scoop up the leaves.

The scene seemed so natural to Rupert, and so beautiful. Why, he wondered? Was it truth? Nature was real and its reality could not be avoided, not by anyone. The weather warms in the spring, the leaves fall in the autumn, tornados twist their way across the midwestern plains in the late summer. Nature is beautiful, he thought. Man must accept and then deal with the reality of nature, if he is to survive happily. The laws of nature could never be abolished or vetoed.

Or, was the beauty of the scene, Rupert wondered, to be found in the fact that the human mind had again figured out how to deal with nature, how to more effectively and easily accomplish the task of picking up leaves.

In the window, Rupert could see the reflection of a woman's face staring at him. He turned around and looked at her.

"Hi," she said.

"Hello."

"You're smiling. That's nice. Not many people smile these days, when they're sitting alone."

"Maybe they don't have much to smile about."

"You do? What makes you so happy?"

"Me."

"Me?"

"Yes. I like who I am. How I feel about myself."

"How do you feel?" she asked.

"That my life is mine to fashion. That no one owns me. That I am what I am and what I can be is up to me and me alone."

"You're lucky," she said, not smiling. "I don't feel that way."

"You could. Anyone could."

"Where do I start?"

"By being totally honest with yourself about who you are and what you want. By being totally honest with others about who you are, what you're thinking, how you feel. By recognizing that your happiness is in your hands and nobody else's. That's the beginning."

"You make it sound easy. Would you help me?"

"You must help yourself first."

She hesitated. "Would you like to have a drink?"

Rupert smiled. "Yes."

As they left the train, Rupert looked but could not see any wire running from one car to the next. Each car must draw electricity from the third rail, he thought. He made a mental note to write to the train company and inquire.

Rupert sat opposite her at a small table in a cafe two blocks from the railroad station.

"What happens," she asked, "if you look inside yourself and you do not like what you see?"

"Change it."

"Sometimes that could be hard to do. Sometimes, maybe, it's too late to change."

"Never too late. What couldn't be changed?"

"I don't know. How you feel about life." Her eyes seemed alert.

"How do you feel about your life right now?" he asked.

"I feel that it should be an incredible high. After all, think of the alternative. But it isn't. I mean it rarely hits that high, and I don't know why."

"The thing I've been able to figure out," said Rupert, "is that it doesn't come to you, you have to go out and get it. You have to decide what it is that will make you happy, really happy down deep and long-range, and then stick to getting that, no matter what. It seems to me that so many people settle for less than they really want. You have to decide that as far as you're concerned, your life is the single most important thing there is, your most precious treasure."

"I wish my husband were more like you," she said. "He never talks to me this way. He doesn't think I can understand anything. I'm not sure he does, either. I know one thing. We're not happy together. I mean, not the way we should be. We sort of play at being happy, as if that's what we should be, but we aren't."

"Have you told him how you feel?"

"No, he wouldn't listen, he wouldn't believe the truth. Would you like to come to my place for another drink? My husband's away and won't be back till next Monday. We could drink and talk and everything. Would you like that?"

"I don't think so."

"No, why not? We could be more comfortable there, if you know what I mean."

"I know what you mean. Tell your husband what you just told me. Maybe he's feeling some of the same things you are."

"Maybe."

"I have to go now," said Rupert. "Enjoyed our chat."

"I think I feel better. Is that possible?"

"You tell me," said Rupert.

* * * * * * * * * *

"Mr. Lyle, when can I expect my equipment?"

"In two months, Mr. McClintock."

"Hah! You mean five, don't you? You guys are all the same, always shaving the delivery time. You say two months and mean five."

"I mean two months."

"Two months would be fine, five months is out. Definitely out."

"It'll be two months, you can believe that."

"You're lying."

Durney had been right, thought Rupert. McClintock would not accept the truth. The implication horrified him. It wasn't the truth that was acceptable anymore, it was something else. It wasn't reality the world wanted to deal with anymore, it was something else. Man had encased himself in a straightjacket and had lost the key. Rupert shuddered at the realization of how close he, himself, had come to losing the key.

"No, I'm not lying, sir."

"Are you calling me a liar, Lyle?"

"No, sir, you're calling me a liar."

"You're insolent, Lyle. No deal. I don't want your equipment. I don't want your lies. I'm canceling the order. Tell Durney."

* * * * * * * * * *

"You're fired, Rupert."

"I know, sir."

"You know?"

"Yes, sir."

"Are you crazy?"

"I don't think so. Not anymore."

"You've just lost your job, Lyle. Doesn't that bother you?"

"Yes, but not as much as losing something else would bother me."

"What something else?"

"Something on my page."

"What page?"

"You wouldn't understand, Mr. Durney."

"You're out of step with the world, Lyle."

"I'm glad to hear that."

"You don't have all your marbles."

"I don't play with marbles anymore."

"You're dangerous, Lyle."

"To whom?"

"To everyone. To me."

"That's true."

"You'll never work again, Lyle, if I have anything to do with it."

"You don't. And I'm working now."

"You are?"

"Yes."

"What are you working at?"

"Me."

"You? What are you talking about?"

"Goodbye...Durney." Rupert turned and began to walk away.

"Answer me, Lyle", screamed Durney. "What in tarnation are you talking about? Where are you going? Come back here. You can keep working, dammit, just straighten yourself out. Get with it. I'll talk to McClintock and work things out. I'll explain to him that you always tell the truth. Cripes, Rupert! What does truth have to do with anything? Come on back, Lyle. Please. Be good."

Rupert didn't answer, except with the corners of his mouth that turned upward into a soft smile.

I'm me at last, Rupert thought to himself. At last, it's me. Truth. Integrity. Pride.

He felt as if a shadowy veil had been lifted from about him and he had emerged from a self-imposed cocoon into glaring sunlight. What had he been afraid of all those years? Why had he hidden within himself? Why had he, so often, given more weight to what others wanted than to what he wanted? Why had he been so concerned about what others thought of him? Was he not master of his own soul, his own life?

Time had been lost, he knew, that he could never recover, but what mattered now was today, and tomorrow. I can and should make of myself what I wish. It's not a question of who will let me; it's a question of who will stop me.

Rupert Lyle had come alive.

THE BEGINNING

www.ingramcontent.com/pod-product-compliance
Lightning Source LLC
Chambersburg PA
CBHW060804050426
42449CB00008B/1525